ADLARD COLES
Bloomsbury Publishing Plc
50 Bedford Square, London, WC1B 3DP, UK
29 Earlsfort Terrace, Dublin 2, Ireland

BLOOMSBURY, ADLARD COLES and
the Adlard Coles logo are trademarks of
Bloomsbury Publishing Plc

First published in Great Britain 2021

ISBN: 978-1-4729-8147-9;
ePUB: 978-1-4729-8146-2;
ePDF: 978-1-4729-8145-5

10 9 8 7 6 5 4 3 2 1

Typeset in Barlow Condensed
Designed by Austin Taylor
Printed and bound in China
by Toppan Leefung Printing

FSC
www.fsc.org
MIX
Paper from
responsible sources
FSC® C104723

To find out more about our authors
and books visit www.bloomsbury.com
and sign up for our newsletters

# CONTENTS

# INTRODUCTION: THE SUP-RISING

Stand-Up Paddleboarding (SUP) is a combination of surfing and canoeing. It has only become popular since the start of the Millennium. Back in 2012 on popular beaches you probably wouldn't have seen more than a couple of paddleboarders. By 2014 it was often referred to as the world's fastest growing watersport and regarded by some as the fastest growing of any type of sport.

Now those beaches could have 100 'Suppers', and lakes, canals and rivers also have their share. Try it a couple of times and you'll hopefully appreciate why. As a keen canoeist and kayaker, I thought: why stand when you can sit? After a couple of clumsy goes, the challenge of remaining on your feet and the satisfaction of thinking – possibly to the tune by Elton John, 'I'm still standing!' – had me, and my toes

*Sport doesn't have to be competitive.*

in particular, well and truly gripped, along with very many other people around the globe.

A bit of guidance would have helped me and I suspect lots of others. Of those 100 people on the beach, it would be no surprise if 20 had their paddles the wrong way around. With a few tips, plenty would be able to paddle in a reasonably straight line or turn efficiently. Hence one reason for writing this book. More than just a comprehensive 'how to' guide, it will hopefully enthuse you about the many ways to enjoy the sport and the various health benefits it brings. It will also describe the

environments it enables people to explore and the wildlife that may be seen (this is my specialism).

There are many helpful tips and explanations in the following pages

*Try to improve your standing in a group.*

*Reach for the stars.*

Aloha! SUP surfers, Kauai, Hawaii.

to improve technique but also other ways to derive more enjoyment from this wonderful activity. These include games and challenges, planning a safe tour based on the weather and tides, along with everything from racing to yoga and anything else that floats your boat (or board).

# A potted past of paddleboarding

Many cultures and parts of the world could claim to have come up with the idea of paddling small canoe-like craft in a standing position. These include Africa, the Middle East, China and South America, with a pre-Incan civilisation in Peru

having a particularly strong claim from 2,000 years ago.

Perhaps writer, artist and lover of the Lake District Beatrix Potter should be credited as the pioneer of paddleboarding. In her charming book *The Tale of Squirrel Nutkin*, published in 1903, the squirrels are pictured and described paddling to Owl Island in a standing position on little rafts. In 1953, inspired by seeing a picture in a magazine of an Australian lifeguard paddling a rectangular board, inventive British carpenter Charlie Force made a board which he paddled in Newquay Bay, Cornwall, laying claim to be the UK's first Supper.

Hawaiians benefit from a consistently clement climate, warm water and wonderful waves, but they certainly made the most of them through their development and mastery of surfing. As Supping is the offspring of canoeing and, perhaps more particularly, surfing, much gratitude must go to them. It is believed that as early as the 16th century they used paddles with large surfboards. In 1995 top surfers in Hawaii including Dave Kalama and Laird Hamilton began Supping as a form of training and had paddles specially made. A decade later SUP was diversifying from surfing into racing, touring, river paddling, yoga and fishing, and by 2006 production SUP boards became available.

*The big SUPrise is that it didn't catch on earlier. Gorran Haven, Cornwall.*

What next? SUP may become an Olympic, Paralympic and Special Olympics sport?

*Inland, calm rivers offer a different experience.*

# 1 BASIC TECHNIQUES

# Equipment

We'll look at 'kit' in more detail later but here's a list of the important bits.

Your board should have a fin or some arrangement of three smaller fins underneath at the back. As a beginner it is far better to learn on an inflatable board. They inflate to be almost as firm as a rigid board, but if the waves smack the edge into your shin or if you fall on them it's unlikely to cause pain.

Attached to the back of your board should be a leash. These should be one flexible length or short and curly (coiled). These not only prevent you from losing your board, but mean a stray board won't take out several other paddlers if you fall. They also connect you to a great buoyancy aid – your board. Use the Velcro to attach the free end to either ankle. Most people put it round the ankle of their dominant side, or if you've tried surfing, the ankle of the foot you tend to put behind you.

You will also need a paddle of the right length to suit you. To start with reach up with one arm – the paddle height should be level with your wrist. Some instructors suggest fanning out your hand with your thumb touching your head – the top of the paddle should come to the top of your little finger. Others recommend holding the paddle upright with the handle downward - eyes should be level with the start of the blade. All three ways give a similar outcome for most people. The ideal length will vary based on the conditions and the sort of paddling you'll be doing.

If you're a complete novice and either the water or air temperatures are relatively low, wearing a wetsuit will help stop you getting cold. It may give you more confidence not to worry about falling in. It will also give you some protection if you fall on your board, which is more of a concern with a rigid board.

Buoyancy aids, which fit like a waistcoat, are recommended, particularly for beginners. Experienced paddlers in a group under calm conditions may choose to keep them handy, for instance clipped to strings on the front of their boards, but novices should wear them and on some bodies of water it is a specified requirement.

# Step by step

Before going into a step by step (or stroke by stroke) approach, let's begin with the two most important tips. These will help you to avoid the two most common mistakes:

● The paddle blade should be angled forward, i.e. furthest away from you toward the bottom. I'll explain why this is more efficient later.
● When you attempt standing up, look ahead of you, not down at your feet. This will make you less likely to fall straight over.

Let's get started:

1 **Begin on your knees** in shallow water, but deep enough that the fins are above the bed with you on the board. Plant each knee evenly shoulder width apart either side of the front end of the handle, with the knee on the far side first. Ideally you want to be in fairly calm water with a safe bed, such as sand.

SUPposition: it's best to have your paddle this way around.

Hand positions when kneeling.

2 **While kneeling,** your higher hand should be around a quarter of the way down the length of your paddle (including blade). Your lower hand should be about a third of the way from the bottom. Note the grip positions on the photograph.

3 **Try a few strokes** on each side. Start with your lower arm almost straight and reaching forward push the whole blade into the water. Try to bring the paddle back alongside your board by

pushing your top arm until it is pretty much straight. When the blade, still fully immersed, comes back level with your hips, lift the blade upwards and sideways out of the water and repeat.

4 **Try not to scrape** or whack the side of your board – the more vertical your paddle shaft the straighter your direction of travel will be. Unless there is wind coming from the side, you will probably soon begin to veer away from the side you're paddling on.

*Wide forward strokes turn you slowly.*

*Wide backward strokes turn you faster.*

*Lake Lucerne, Switzerland – admire the view as you stand up to avoid a Swiss roll.*

**5** **After three or four strokes,** transfer your paddle to the other side. You need to swap your hands so they each go where the other one was – then resume paddling. It is possible to paddle in a straight line without swapping, though this will be explained in the 'Advanced Techniques' chapter (*see page 30*).

**6** **Try doing a wide stroke.** Experiment to see the effects of fairly wide strokes and taking the stroke as wide as you can to the side. This will enable you to change direction, but if you wanted to turn around 180° it would take several strokes. A faster way to turn is a wide backward stroke on the side you want to turn toward, pushing the blade forward. Start with your paddle blade near the back of your board, bring it round in a wide arc to the front of the board with the usual front of the blade first. With a reasonably manoeuvrable board this will turn you about 90°. Repeat if needed.

# Become a stand-up paddler
## – a pop-up guide

An exciting moment for anyone taking up SUP is the first time you try to stand up.

Before breaking the process down, take a moment to remember the tip: look ahead as you stand up – if you look down you'll probably fall down. This is because your head is quite heavy – about one seventh of your total body weight. Aside from how heavy your head is, it's about four times further from the board than your knees, so it has four times the effect on your balance.

Beginners may find it helps to practise on a board or imaginary board at home while following these steps.

1 · BASIC TECHNIQUES

11

**1** Begin on your knees.

**2** **Paddle enough** to get a little momentum going. This can help with balance, like riding a bike.

**3** Assume a male gorilla pose.

**4** **Place one foot in position,** then the other so you're squatting. You're aiming to have your feet either side of the handle, about shoulder width apart with heels slightly turned inward.

**5** **Reposition your hands:** The top hand should be over the handle and the other around halfway down the shaft. (If you hold your arms up above your head with elbows bent at right angles, this will give you the distance apart your hands should be.)

**6** **Now remembering where to look** (ahead/horizon), steadily stand up, though your knees should be slightly bent, and gently start paddling.

If you have had knee or back problems or feel you lack balance, SUP will really help, but you may need extra help. If you're tall and/or broad your centre of gravity will be higher. Your weight in relation to the board will also be a factor. I've taught couples where the woman is a slight 5ft 2in and the man is a sporty 6ft 5in with shoulders to match. She feels she's finally found a sport that suits her as he normally takes longer to master the balance.

One way to help somebody who is struggling is to find waist deep water and hold the back of their board while they get to their feet. (Persuade a friend to do this if you're struggling.) As they get used to standing, gradually apply less steadying force to the board.

At first keep the strokes gentle and keep looking ahead, possibly to the horizon. As you begin to feel more comfortable and balanced you can paddle

*Assume the gorilla pose.*

*Place one foot level with the handle, then the other.*

*Look ahead and steadily stand in a slight squat.*

more purposefully. As with kneeling, swap arms every few strokes as required.

If you feel a wobble or a wave coming, lower your centre of gravity by squatting more and leaning forward, not by hunching your back. You can also steady yourself if you twist your paddle outwards and press the blade reasonably flat against the water surface. This is known as a support stroke. It is best to meet waves at right angles or at least avoid being parallel with them, which would make you wobble more.

Once you're feeling more confident, try deliberately wobbling your board by pressing your feet down alternately and adjusting your balance. This will develop the reflexes you need to stay standing. It's also good practice for one of the games in the next chapter!

Don't be afraid of falling off. Horse riding instructors sometimes say 'you're not a proper rider until you've fallen off' and it's the same with SUP. Once people have had their first tumble, they tend to relax more.

Try falling off deliberately. The best way is to fall backward with your head tucked in slightly and your paddle held out horizontally in front of you. This works well as a practice and it's good to get used to it. However, in the moment when you suddenly think you might fall, you'll probably try to save your balance. You may recover, fall forward or step off. This is another reason why it's less painful to learn on an inflatable board.

# The stroke

- The ideal stroke involves reaching forward with your back straight, squatting more as you reach, and starting with your lower arm almost straight.
- Push the paddle down with a digging motion so the whole blade is underwater. This is known as the **'catch'**.
- As soon as the blade is fully submerged, begin pushing forward with the top hand, using your chest and shoulder muscles and almost straightening your top arm, while pulling back with the lower arm, using your back muscles. Your top arm should be at around 90° to your body. This is called the **'power phase'**. Think of it as moving your board forward, rather than your paddle backward.
- Once the blade is level with your heel pull it out upwards and sideways (the **'exit'**), your upper hand moves round a bit like turning a steering wheel until the blade is just out of the water, then reach forward (the **'recovery phase'**) and begin again.

Dig the full blade in for the catch.

Exit the blade smoothly near your heel.

# Why does the paddle go that way around?

Many people SUP with the paddle the wrong way around and the way the paddles are designed to be held may seem counter-intuitive. This may be because when you first reach forward and plant the blade in with your paddle the wrong way around, the blade is vertical and its full force can be applied to the water. However as soon as you start bringing the paddle back it becomes less forceful. Then when you bring it out you have to lift an angled blade against resistance from the water splashing inefficiently. By contrast, if you have it aligned correctly with the blade pointing toward the front of the board:

● You can reach more water.
● Gradually the blade becomes more vertical, helping you to apply more power and accelerate.
● This puts less of a sudden strain on your shoulders.
● Once the blade is back level with your heel it can be lifted from the water with very little resistance or splashing.

# Common faults

● Paddle held the wrong way around as explained above.
● Pulling the paddle back too far: If it goes beyond your heel it provides little forward thrust in relation to effort and there will be more water resistance when taking it out. Pushing up water with the blade behind will also drive the board deeper into the water, slowing you down.
● Hands too close together and not straightening your arms enough: This is OK for pootling down a river but means you don't get the benefit from (and to) the larger muscles of your chest, shoulders and back, but your arms tire out much more.
● Not squatting: Again, fine for gentle cruising, but you'll be less balanced, less able to react if needed, and won't reach as far with your strokes, which will be less effective.
● Not swapping hand positions when swapping your paddle to the other side: Some beginners make this mistake, but it is ineffective and looks very awkward.
● Not gripping the handle when standing: Some people paddle very proficiently with their upper hand below the handle and

we're all different, but generally it's better to wrap your fingers over the handle so you can use them to drive the blade down and direct it, while using the lower part of your top hand to push the handle forward.

• Standing too far from the centre may not help your balance. However, if you're paddling into the wind it's better to stand a little further forward to keep the nose down. Paddling with the wind, stand a little further back to keep the rear down. Where the sea gradually becomes shallower over a long distance, standing further forward can enable you to paddle in slightly shallower water as your fin will come up a little.

# Stopping

A quick short backward paddle along each side of your board will help you to come to a stop – very useful!

# Pride comes before a fall. After it comes getting back on

In calm shallow water getting back on your board is fairly easy. Getting back on when you take a tumble in deep water takes more effort, and if you have to do it more than once in quick succession it can be quite tiring. At first this became my main skill! Many people work out a way for themselves, but here's how step by step:

1 **Grab your paddle** and place it on top of the far side of your board, lengthways toward the front.

2 **Approach the side** of your board just behind the handle.

3 **Hold the handle** with the hand nearest the front.

4 **Grab the far side** with your other hand and at the same time try to hoist as much of your body weight over the board as you can without tipping it over. You may have to grab the far side of the board with both hands and do a bit of front crawl swimming kick to achieve this, and it may take more than one attempt.

5 **Once you have** your chest over the board, while pulling with your arms, swing your legs onto the back of the board.

*This is harder in cold water but remain calm.*

*Swim kick your legs.*

*Made it!*

15

Once safely on your board:

1 **Make sure you feel OK** if you aren't already aware of any injuries. Rescues and tows will be covered in the 'Advanced Techniques' chapter.

2 **Assume the kneeling position.** If you're tired don't stand up until you've at least got your breath back.

3 **Don't be deterred.** Stand up again once you're ready. All the best paddlers have taken a tumble and most still do occasionally. If you've never fallen in, you haven't really immersed yourself in the activity!

# An initial word on wind

Sooner or later we all encounter problems from wind.

**If it becomes windy:** Squat more to lower your centre of gravity and engage your legs more to help you balance. You may also want to shorten your paddle slightly (maybe 5cm).

**If it gets very windy:** Go down to either high or low kneeling. You'll be more stable,

*Place the paddle blade under your chest for prone paddling.*

and if going into the wind your body will act less like a sail, which would slow you more if standing.

**If it gets downright ridiculous:** Lay your paddle down on the board with the handle forward and the blade front face upwards, so you can lie down with your chest over the blade. That way you'll be well balanced and won't lose your paddle if the water is choppy. It also enables you to hold your board if a big wave arrives. Swim with your arms, either front crawl to go forward or one arm pushing forward and one backward to turn. Butterfly will give you more power and an excellent shoulder workout! Head to safety.

This 'prone paddling' can also be useful if your paddle breaks. This is fairly rare with good paddles but can happen,

*Kneeling into the wind in Snowdonia.*

Back-paddling: you can't do this in a canoe.

particularly with cheaper ones. If you fall off and your paddle drifts away, remount and prone paddle to retrieve it.

One of the great things about teaching is that sometimes someone will try something somewhat original. On one stag group tour, the groom lay on his back and paddled. I tried it and was surprised how effective it seemed. On a long windy paddle trying different positions can vary the muscles used and help prevent muscle fatigue.

When prone paddling is necessary, on your front is the norm, though you may see more of what's going on around you if face up. Either way, between you and your group, keep a look out for boats and other hazards.

Wind will be explained in more detail later (*see page 132*). Before going anywhere more challenging, build up your skills and find organised groups or experienced friends to accompany you.

You may find shelter in the lee of sea walls or riverbank bends and vegetation. Don't paddle near walls or cliffs that aren't sheltered as you may get blown into them. Also as waves bounce off a wall they can combine with the waves coming toward the wall to be almost double their height. This applies to big rounded waves as well as small choppy ones.

It may sound obvious, but even when going a short distance, it's best to start heading into the wind and come back with the help of the wind. You may be tired and it will help you get back quicker, especially if there's a problem. When paddling with the wind, if you want a rest you can raise your paddle with the blade high above you so the wind blows on the blade and gives you a little help. Lengthen adjustable paddles for greater effect. You'll appreciate why sails were invented. One friend takes an umbrella and sits down with it open!

Paddling with a side wind can be hard too. You might not have to change paddling sides much but this can be tiring. As mentioned before, you'll remain more stable if you meet waves at right angles but waves parallel to your board are most likely to knock you off. It can be worth zig-zagging to avoid this to some extent.

Not just useful on rainy days.

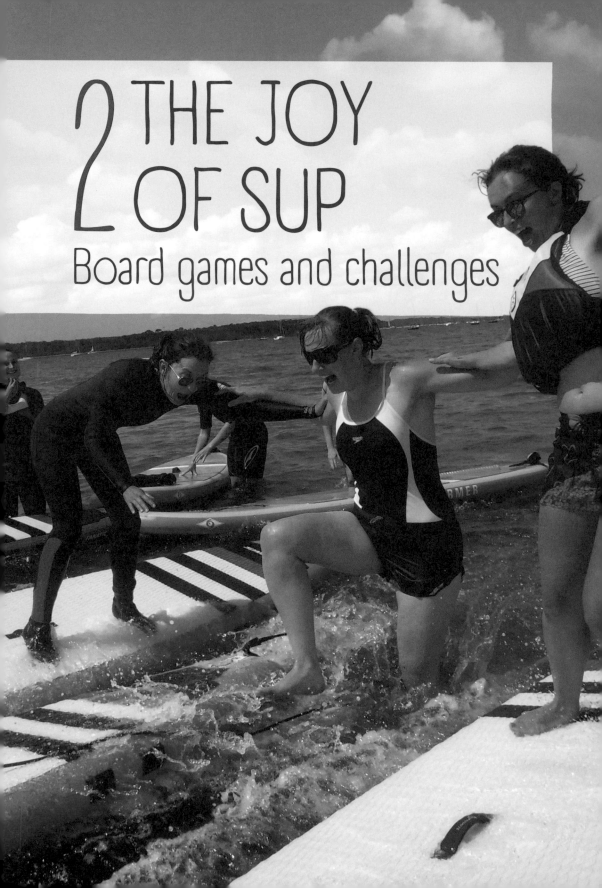

# 2 THE JOY OF SUP

## Board games and challenges

That's enough straightforward paddling to be going on with. If you're new to paddleboarding you may feel saturated with technique. You may get soaked now, but it's time for some fun!

All of the following games and challenges develop balance, reflexes, confidence and useful skills as well as being enjoyable. This will help when it comes to advancing your technique in the next chapter. Inflatable boards are preferable for games, being less injurious and less easily damaged. Please take care and play at your own risk.

# One-board wonders

Let's begin with ideas that only require one board:

1 **Wobble board** – possibly the most popular game. You may remember deliberate wobbling was recommended to develop leg reflexes and balance. Now it's time to test those skills. Undo the leashes and put your paddles somewhere safe. Two people kneel at either end of the same board facing each other. One of you or a third person (umpire) says '1, 2, 3 stand' and both stand. An umpire, if available, can also hold the middle of the board steady as you stand. When they or one of you shouts 'wobble', you both wobble your legs and weight until one or both falls off. The winner is the last one standing. Draws aren't unusual. Try to resist physical contact; it may be an easy win but it shouldn't be a 'push-over'! As you may find, it's slightly easier at the back end where the grip is better and the fins may add to stability, so swap around and go again.

It's fun to come up with your own variations of challenges. You could try facing away from each other if you have an umpire or just one of you turn away if you keep winning.

1. Flossing helps; no grabbing, wobble not knobble!

Falling about laughing about falling.

2. United we stand...

...divided we fall.

2. It was his birthday! This may bring you closer together.

water to try this, in case of falling in. See whether you can turn on your board to face the back, taking a couple of steps with each foot.

4 **180° jump** – now try this with a jump. You might find this easier than stepping – if you land well balanced.

5 **360° jump** – if you want more of a challenge. Holding your paddle like a tight-rope walker's pole may help. Use your hips to generate enough spin.

6 **Knee leap** – the classic trampoline leap from a kneeling position to standing on your feet works well on a board.

4. and 5. Might as well jump... go ahead and jump!

2 **Stand up across the board** – for this two people kneel facing each other on either side of the handle (i.e. across the middle of the board, not at either end). Hold each other's hands or forearms and try to both rise to a standing position.

For a much easier alternative, face each other at either side of the handle along its length. You could then suddenly switch to a combative game of wobble board. The readiness of some people, particularly couples, to dramatically turn from friend to foe can be surprising.

3 **180° turn** – you may want a good couple of feet (60cm or so) depth of

7. How hard can it be?

10. Supside down!

**7** **Stand on one leg** – harder than it sounds. Standing on your toes is testing too and standing on the toes of one foot is another level. You can lean on your paddle with it upright in front of you and lift it once you feel steady.

8. Singing 'la-la, la-la-la-la, la-la' is just an option.

**8** **We all stand together** – with a group, you could try this variation: put your paddles to one side and arrange your boards parallel to each other. Put your hands around each other's shoulders while kneeling and try to stand up together. Every other person can stand on one leg, then just the others, then attempt all together. Try raising your knees high, then the whole straight leg. This takes a 'can do' approach and can take on a 'cancan' appearance!

9. The bridge in a suitable setting.

**9** **Bridge or back-bend** – best to warm up and stretch first. We'll look at SUP Yoga later.

**10** **Headstand** – I found it helped to practise on a trampoline. Having a six-year-old insist on bouncing around me added to the challenge. Holding the sides of your board helps.

**11** **Handstands** – there are various options including athletic yoga positions and gymnastic feats.

**12** **Step onto your board / jump on it** – in shallow water, with a safe bed, try to step from the bed straight into standing on your board, far leg first. Now try jumping directly onto the board. Which do you find harder? If you land well it may be the latter, which is good for the reflexes.

**13** **Skipping on a board with a rope** is another option: see how many you can do.

**14** **Ballet** – a ballerina I took for her initial lesson suggested a pirouette. Sadly it was too windy and choppy for her to try that day, but she clearly had amazing balance. Transferable skills can be very useful. Try a Plié or an Arabesque and release your inner ballet dancer!

Who needs a pommel horse?

15. To floss, perform a mad wriggle!

**16 Paddle backward** – turning around on your board will make this more efficient so the nose is still heading forward. It will be easier after you've mastered the skills in the 'Advanced Techniques' chapter. It's a fine activity to develop strength and flexibility. It can also be a way of looking out for people behind you, though they may rib you for showing off, especially if you fall in.

**17 All aboard** – see how many people can sit or stand on one board.

**15 Dance** – there is definitely an opening for all manner of SUP dance or Zumba classes. Flossing works well on a board. Twerking isn't for everyone, but 'Gangnam style' and the Macarena are particularly good challenges. Take care with the 'C' in 'YMCA'!

*Combining 15 and 17:
Oops SUP side your head!*

19. See which board you prefer, without dismounting.

18. Try a triangle.

# Games for more boards

With more boards you could try:

**18** **Take shape** – a good steering exercise is for three people to form a perfect triangle. Larger numbers can form polygons with more sides.

**19** **Board swap** – two people swap boards while standing. This is tricky and to do it by jumping doesn't make it any easier. Facing each other and stepping one foot at a time helps.

**20** **Welcome on board** – mount your board on the back of one in front. To achieve this: ask them to stay still; come up straight behind them with some momentum; step far enough back on your board for the front to rise and lodge it on the back of their board; then step forward to the middle and paddle/push them along. This can be a useful way for a strong paddler to help someone who is struggling or tired, though this is more likely in tough conditions when it is harder to accomplish a good position.

**21** **Tandem paddling** – arrange one board with the front over the back of another board, covering the handle. The person in front kneels on the front of their board and the person behind (ideally the heavier one, and the one with long enough legs) sits astride the wide part of both boards with legs gripping the sides, but not dangling. This can be a real saviour if you have to head into a strong wind as it combines the power of both of you.

21. Stand or straddle as you paddle.

24. Parallel paddling: The most sociable way to SUP.

**22** **Caterpillar or centipede** – use either 20 or 21 to make longer arrangements of boards.

**23** **Trains** – one person paddles a bendy route, the others have to follow the person in front of them as best they can in a snaking line.

**24** **Parallel paddling** – this can be a particularly sociable way to paddle standing or kneeling. It's easiest with similar boards. Two paddlers come alongside each other, boards touching and paddle on the far side of each board.

This means you won't have to change arms, though you could swap positions after a while. This is another fun skill that can be particularly useful if one paddler is struggling to steer. If this is because of a cross wind, have the stronger paddler on the downwind side.

22. Watch out for the domino effect.

25 **Races/relays** – pick a route with buoys as turning points. These can involve tandem paddling, standing, kneeling or prone paddling, as well as combinations of these in a relay. The finish can require touching a buoy with a paddle, high fiving a 'race official' who could move slightly to favour weaker paddlers, or a line between two people, buoys or other markers. For an extra challenge, contestants have to start by touching the very front of their boards with their chins, which is more troublesome than it sounds.

26 **Raft building** – arrange your boards in a raft or pyramid by crossing boards one way then the other. Avoid having fins digging into other boards. Be careful not to press boards down on paddles as they can break. All clamber on and paddle or have one or two people pushing. Lying on top can be very relaxing. Human pyramids kneeling on top of each other can be less relaxing but a good challenge. Make sure you're in deep

26. I won't go down with this ship.

enough water before anyone decides to leap off, especially if back flipping.

Rafts can also be used for fun races, with losing teams having to perform dances mentioned in 15 as embarrassing forfeits, though they are easier on a raft. The cancan can be done in a circle.

*An advanced party from the Army tries a tougher arrangement.*

27. Pick the next runner before you're too dizzy.

28. Keep it under wraps, but overlaps are easier.

**27** **Run around** – you can also take it in turns to run around a circle of people on a raft: choose your replacement, pat them on the shoulder and swap.

Finally, there are a few games that are definitely best done with inflatable boards.

**28** **Run across boards** – put your paddles securely on one board. Arrange all the other boards side on, parallel to each other in water deep enough so that you can all stand comfortably with your heads and shoulders above the surface. Half of the group should stand on each side, with everyone holding a couple of boards together to keep the arrangement steady. Take it in turns to run across the boards. You can also jump from board to board, go backward or imitate a crab sideways. Jump with

style at the end, but make sure there's a good depth of water for any acrobatics. Waggling the boards makes it very hard.

You can also have races with two people. A megaSup (a very large board designed for several people) makes a great starting platform.

A variation is to overlap the boards slightly like roof slates. This makes them easier to hold together and if you start from the top board it's easier to run across.

*Serious training for our Forces personnel.*

**29 Circle of trust** – if you have quite a few boards, these can be arranged in a circle with each person kneeling across two boards, one knee on each. If you try standing across two boards each, you may end up doing the splits. People can take turns at running around the outside as on rafts.

**30 What time is it, Mr. Wolf?** – the wolf faces away and others advance toward them, three strokes when the wolf calls 3 o'clock and so on. This is a good way to promote and practise fast turns at 'dinner time' or perhaps the wolf should shout 'Supper time'!

*Supball is a popular sport at Manly Wharf, Sydney, the home of Supball. It takes flat water Supping to a whole new level!*

# Games with frontiers

Some games are best played when you can set boundaries such as buoys:

**31 Tag** – like ordinary 'tag', someone is 'on' and every time they touch someone's board with their paddle that person is on also. The last person to be tagged wins.

**32 Last person standing** – like Tag but you have to knock each other's' boards so they fall down. A bit rougher, so try not to hurt each other.

**33 Ultimate SUP Frisbee** – two teams within boundaries have to throw the frisbee to team mates until one member of the attacking team catches the frisbee in their 'end zone'. If a member of the opposition team catches it they have possession and try to pass it between them until it's caught in their end zone. If it falls in the water the first person to grab it gains possession for their side. You can use paddles to try to intercept it in mid-air. After one team scores,

*Reedmace*    *Kingfisher*    *Dragonfly*

*Minnow*    *Swan*    *Alder*

*Moorhen*    *Water Crowfoot*    *Coot*

35. *Wildlife bingo cards.*

the other team starts from the end zone they were defending, or swap around if conditions favour one direction. This can get a little physical too.

**34** **SUP Polo** – various versions similar to above but with a ball and goals instead of end zones. There are even organised tournaments with specially designed paddles.

Finally for something completely different that may work well with younger paddlers:

**35** **Wildlife Bingo** – make cards, preferably laminated, showing photos of nine plants, birds or animals you might see on a paddle, arranged in a 3 × 3 square. Players try to spot as many as they can or complete a horizontal, vertical or diagonal line of three species. The wildlife chapter (*see page 68*) could help with ideas.

**36** **Scavenger hunt** – make a list of things to find, like alder catkins and willow leaves.

2 • THE JOY OF SUP

29

# 3 ADVANCED TECHNIQUES

# Why is good technique useful?

Once you've mastered the basics and you feel comfortable on your board, it's time to hone your technique. You won't want to go full speed all the time, but there are several reasons why efficient paddling may be necessary or beneficial. You may want to enter a race, there may be an emergency or conditions may become tough, with strong winds or currents, or you may simply be running late.

# Steering and turning strokes

Two skills are particularly important.

## Going straight

Firstly, paddle in a straight line. The more vertical your paddle, the straighter your course will be. At the start of the stroke you should briefly be looking through the gap under your top arm. Swapping arms can break your momentum slightly. A good vertical stroke may mean you can paddle a few more strokes on each side before needing to.

The really useful but slightly tricky bit is called the bow stroke (this is pronounced like the front of a ship, as in 'now' – some paddlers call it the J-stroke). It's called the bow stroke because you bring the paddle toward the front (bow) of your board.

*Good technique could help you join a party on time!*

- Use the usual grip, but instead of digging the paddle in with the back of the blade facing you, twist your wrist outward so the back of the blade faces toward your board, near the front of the rail (side of your board).
- Leave a gap between the blade and the board of between 30 and 45cm. You'll feel slightly more of a stretch under your upper armpit.
- Once the blade is fully immersed, use your paddle as a fulcrum to pull the front of your board toward it, closing the gap between blade and board.

*Paddle well with pace in a rush or race.*

On the water try paddling in a straight line, maybe parallel to a sea wall or toward a pair of buoys, keeping them in line. With practice you'll only need a hint of a bow stroke with each stroke or a good one if you start to veer.

On a river you should be able to cope with small curves in direction without changing paddling sides. Try to use both sides equally, even if you have a favourite side (try not to have one!) Sometimes a side-wind may mean you have to paddle predominantly on one side. At least with this technique you can have a small break with a few bow strokes on the other side.

Canoeists rely on a stroke with a J-shaped curve behind them, twisting the

*The 'bow stroke'.*

- As you do this, start to untwist your wrist as you pull the blade toward you, with the bottom of the shaft performing a J-shaped motion.
- See how this adjustment compensates for the board's tendency to veer away from your paddle side. It may even overcompensate.
- Now try with less of a wrist twist, perhaps 45°, and practise so the movement and particularly the J-shape becomes smooth, not just a sudden adjustment at the start of the stroke. The second half of the stroke is as normal.

*Dig your blade in at this angle with a gap between blade and board.*

wrist so the back of the blade turns away from them once it's beyond them. This is termed the J-stroke. As a paddleboarder you have greater leverage and you wouldn't normally need to bring the paddle behind you. However, if you end up on a board with no fin, you may need to combine the bow stroke with a J-stroke just to keep straight. This is called the C-stroke as the paddle shaft comes around in a C-shaped curve.

# Turning

Now you need to perfect your turning strokes.

Wide strokes turn you quite slowly. Wide backward strokes turn you faster but you lose all your forward momentum. Fortunately there are a couple of better ways to change direction.

### A. THE TWIST TURN

This is the way I usually turn. It is quick and fairly stable. Sometimes it's called the bow cross turn or reverse paddle turn. For this:

1 **Keep your feet and grip** on the paddle as normal.

2 **If paddling on the left** and you wish to turn right, twist your torso so both arms are on the right.

3 **Plant your blade** in the water level with your feet, with the back of the blade facing forward and as wide out from your board as you can easily reach. Squatting more may help.

4 **Bring the paddle round** in a wide arc until the back of the blade is alongside your board near the front of the right side.

Torso twist.

Arc round.

Wide stroke to finish.

**5** **Follow this up** with a wide stroke on the left. This should be a continuation of a smooth wide curve. If you have a very short board it could be one continuous movement around the front of your board. With a reasonably manoeuvrable board you should have turned round 180°.

You may need to develop your suppleness, strength and balance to do this easily. With practice and possibly a little yoga (see later), this should come. If you only need to turn say 120° or not as sharply, you can tone down the range of movement accordingly.

Turn your torso so the back of your blade faces forward, then fully immerse it.

Slam it to the left, if you're having a left turn!

## B. STEP BACK TURN, SOMETIMES CALLED THE PIVOT TURN

This is a good challenge even if you end up favouring the twist turn. It involves moving on the board so it's excellent for developing balance and helps keep the circulation in your feet.

When moving on your board, try to ease the weight off your feet fairly evenly rather than leaning heavily on one foot, as this way the board and you remain better balanced. It takes a bit of practice and the confidence that comes with this. You will probably find it easier to do a 180° jump rather than gradually stepping around to face backward on your board, for this reason. Practise in a situation where it doesn't matter whether you fall in, maybe toward the end of a paddle tour. You can even try the moves on the floor at home.

1 **Turn one foot** in a little across your board, though not over the middle line and be careful not to catch it in or on the board handle.

Move your feet back then apply more weight on your back foot to bring the front of the board up.

2 **As you do this** take the other foot further back along your board, again slightly to the side of the middle line, but on the opposite side.

3 **Now step or shuffle** your feet a bit further back, putting more weight on your back foot until the front of your board rises out of the water a little, so there will be less water resistance when the board turns.

4 **A good wide stroke** will now turn the board fast as you pivot on the back of your board.

5 **With practice** you'll find where the best places to have your feet are for balance and speed, sometimes referred to as the 'sweet spot'. This will vary from person to person and from board to board.

6 **Once the turn** is complete reverse your foot movements to return to the normal SUP stance.

Which is faster? If you're an experienced surfer or develop that kind of balance, the step back may be fractionally faster. However, in a sprint race around a buoy even good paddlers stepping back can fall in and others often do, with the adrenalin pumping and other boards and paddles jostling for position. The first sharp turn can give the pack a good shuffle.

With practice, the twist turn can be very fast and by remaining stable you can sneak through the carnage and kerfuffle unruffled. This is particularly good if you can reach the race marker buoy on the inside of your competitors, as your key turning stroke will be on the inside of the bend, unimpeded by others who will have to take a wider line.

*All you need do is step back and turn...*

*...with wide strokes.*

# Other strokes

There are a few other strokes canoeists use that may be helpful sometimes.

## BOW RUDDER

This can be useful when:
- Gently steering on a river, particularly downstream.
- At sea with a bit of tide or wind, when waiting or resting in a group, to avoid knocking into each other.

Place your blade in the water near the front of your board at right angles to the surface (not flat) and try waggling it like a rudder one way and the other. When pushing it away from your board the board will turn a little away from the paddle. Bringing it toward the board will lever the board toward the paddle.

*Immerse your blade fully at this angle and waggle it to steer.*

*Stern rudder will steer you without stalling your momentum.*

## STERN RUDDER

You can also do the bow rudder while kneeling to go under low branches or bridges, piers or sea arches. However, on your knees you can also do a similar stroke behind you, known as the **stern rudder**, which will have less of a slight stalling effect on your forward momentum. Be sure to duck down as much as you need to! You may even need to prone paddle or take a different route, especially when sea waves are taking you up and down.

*The draw stroke.*

Draw your board toward the paddle. The arrow shows the direction of force on the blade.

There might be times when you want to move your board sideways, perhaps when coming alongside a jetty or canal bank. With forethought you may be able to steer gracefully toward it but, with a current and/or in a group, a sideways movement may be helpful. There are two ways to do this.

The **draw stroke** is the most basic.

1 **Reach out a little way** from your board and place your blade fully in the water with the back of it facing toward your board handle. Your top arm should be reasonably extended.

2 **Lean your opposite hip out** to keep you balanced.

3 **By pulling toward** your paddle, your board will move sideways toward it.

4 **Take the blade out** and repeat as necessary.

5 **Experiment** by having the blade slightly in front or behind you to compensate for current. Try angling your paddle slightly to get a feel for how this affects the board's movement.

The **sculling draw** is similar but more sophisticated. With this you draw the blade toward you from the side to move you sideways, but you do it with a figure of eight motion. It's actually more like a diablo or angular hourglass shape as you pull straight toward you from the far end of each diagonal sweep. The blade stays in the water.

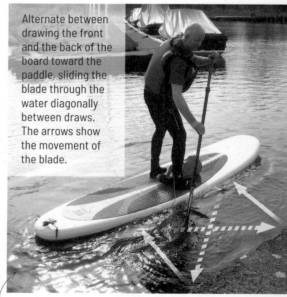

Alternate between drawing the front and the back of the board toward the paddle, sliding the blade through the water diagonally between draws. The arrows show the movement of the blade.

*Slide your paddle down and wind it all around.*

1 **Keeping the shaft fairly vertical,** glide the blade diagonally outward so that the back faces your board a little in front of your handle.

2 **Then use your paddle** as a fulcrum to pull your board toward.

3 **Now glide it diagonally** so that the back faces your board a little way behind your handle.

4 **Again, pull your board toward** the paddle.

5 **The board shouldn't move** as you glide the paddle, only as you pull toward it.

6 **Vary the distance** you slide it away either in front or behind your handle to see how that affects the steering.

This is a similar movement to paddling a traditional coracle. Try to perfect this in calm water to get the feel of it over several repetitions on both sides. If there's a straight waterside near you it will help you see how the steering is going.

If you are paddling alone and one of your arms becomes injured, it is possible to **paddle with one arm** by placing the handle slightly behind your head and bracing the upper shaft against the front of your shoulder. Use your good arm as you would your lower arm as best you can and lever the paddle using your shoulder, near your neck, as a fulcrum. You can stand or kneel and with practice it becomes reasonably effective.

# Top tips for efficient paddling

## Hips and feathers

Now you have the knowledge to steer your board however you choose, you just need to fine tune your normal stroke. Once you have the balance there are a few extra modifications and points to perfect in order to paddle as efficiently as possible.

Firstly, use the power from your **hips**. If you've ever been taught how to throw a cross jab punch, it's important to twist in such a way that your hips provide extra power. The same can apply to paddling.

To achieve this, start your stroke with the knee nearest the paddle further forward and finish with the other knee ahead. That way with a twist of the hips as you come into the stroke you can

*With practice the hip action flows naturally.*

*Feathering reducing wind resistance.*

*This paddler will feel more wind resistance!*

generate more power than just using upper body muscles. Try to keep the paddle vertical and practise on both sides until the action flows.

Secondly, **feather** the paddle. Rowers twist their oars to reduce air resistance when the blades are out of the water. You'll see this on the University Boat Race. As it's been running since 1829, with some top brains as well as brawn, they must have worked out that it's worth it.

In between strokes you have to lift SUP paddle blades and move them through the air. This is known as the 'recovery phase'. With a small twist you can cut the air, rather than forcing the whole width of the blade against it. Over a number of strokes this can save time and energy, particularly when you're heading into the wind.

Here's how: as you lift your blade from the water, twist your wrist so the front of the blade faces down as you bring it

forward. Then untwist to enter the water as you would normally.

Paddling fast can be particularly hard work for the muscles of the higher arm and that shoulder. In the recovery phase, don't raise the arm more than you have to in order to clear the water surface and any waves. If your lower arm takes more of the strain in this movement it can support your higher arm, leaving it stronger for the catch and the power or drive phase. Breathing in and briefly relaxing your upper arm muscles and grip on the recovery stroke will help you with endurance.

Try learning these modifications separately. At first they'll feel a little strange, but with practice in easy conditions you may be surprised at how flowing the moves become. Now you have to combine and integrate them into everything else.

# Summary for fast, efficient paddle strokes

1 **Squat as you reach forward,** keeping your back straight and abdominal muscles stretched (as shown below).

2 **Start by forcefully digging** the top hand down (the catch) to get the whole blade submerged, with your lower arm almost straight. You should briefly be looking through the gap below your higher arm and above your lower arm.

3 **Push forward** with your higher arm, using the power of your shoulder, chest and hips.

4 **Almost straighten the higher arm,** while using your back muscles to pull the lower arm back.

5 **It may help** to breathe out as you stroke.

6 **Slide the paddle out** near your heel, breathe in and feather the blade as you bring it forward.

*Briefly look under your arm, trim if required!*

7 **Stand a little further forward** when paddling into the wind and back a bit when the wind is behind you.

8 **Use bow strokes** to reduce hand swapping.

9 **A fast, shorter stroke** immediately after a hand swap can help keep up the momentum.

*The Fleet, the lagoon along Chesil Beach, Dorset.*

**10** **Try to paddle quietly.** You sometimes see unaccomplished swimmers using a lot of energy as they thrash and splash. Quiet, smooth strokes are a good indication that you aren't wasting effort. If you try paddling almost silently on a river, but not fast, you'll see and hear more wildlife.

Try to fit at least a couple of sprints on both sides into most paddles, if it doesn't detract from an enjoyable paddle with friends. On long fast-paced paddles or races, try to achieve a rhythmic flowing efficient stroke.

*A backward stroke followed by a quick twist and a backward stroke along the other side of your board (as shown) is the most effective way to stop; repeat if necessary.*

## Skills practice

Once you've mastered more advanced technique, some of the challenges in the previous chapter should be less challenging.

Paddling backward, which is easier with the board still pointing forward but you facing backward, can be practised in a couple of ways.

You can alternate between backward strokes on one side and twist turn backward strokes on the other. For the latter use the same torso twist as a twist turn but stroke backward along the side of your board, instead of reaching away from it. This is also a good way to stop or slow down if needed when heading forward.

The other way to paddle backward is to use your paddle as if you were doing bow strokes facing forward, except you're facing the back. This may seem a little awkward and you won't have quite the same range of movement, but it can work well.

Another way to test your new-found skills is to set yourself a slalom course, maybe along a line of buoys. Try snaking through them in one direction then back in the other, but just paddle on one side. You'll have to work out which side to have the paddle on so you can make the 180° turn at the end. Now try with the

paddle on the other side.

Make up your own challenges that involve moving around on the board, like step back turns. This will be easier if you've previously mastered surfing or windsurfing. Remember to try to apply your weight to both feet as evenly as you can.

# Passengers

It can be fun and occasionally useful to take a passenger on board. It works well with a light child but can be a struggle with two average or large adults on a medium sized board. The bigger the board the better. One person, preferably the lighter, kneels or sits toward the front of the board, trying to remain well balanced if not completely still. The other stands or

SUP Yoga taxi service.

kneels a little further back than normal. Experiment to find the best positions that leave the board level.

It's best to be reasonably accomplished for this. Grabbing the front person if you wobble may be fun but accidentally whacking their head with the paddle is anything but.

Some dogs seem to enjoy a ride, but it doesn't appeal to all and obviously shouldn't be done under duress. The size of the dog and how comfortable they are with you are factors. It is best to build up gradually and isn't advisable if going far from shore on the open sea. There are buoyancy aids for dogs. Some canines remain calm on a doggy paddle, some find the motion relaxing, others like to move a lot. Plan breaks as the dog may be thoughtfully trying bladder control.

Pup on a SUP.

# Tows and rescues

If someone is struggling but feeling OK, one way to help is to tow them. Detach the leash from your ankle and attach it to the loop on the board of the person you're helping. If they have a front loop this is straightforward, but if they only have one at the back (more usual), they will have to turn around. They can kneel or sit and help by paddling if they're able, or lie down. As it can be a little jerky, you're better off kneeling. Check they are alright frequently and reassure them if necessary. Make sure the leash remains attached.

You can rescue someone in difficulty in the water using your board:

1 **Climb off your board** and approach them with your board upside down in front of you. Then they can grab your board (and not you, which can be dangerous if they're in a desperate state).

2 **Pull or arrange their arms** over your board a little toward the front, where it is slightly narrower.

3 **If they are able,** they could hold the paddle alongside the board.

4 **Holding the far side** of your board, pull it toward you and brace your feet against it on top of your side so you're squatting. This takes some effort and you'll probably have to brace your knees first unless you're very agile.

5 **Drive with your legs** as if to straighten them.

6 **Eventually the momentum** will bring the board over with the person being rescued on top of it.

7 **Pull their legs** around and arrange them so they are lying comfortably.

8 **Tuck your paddle** safely alongside of them, though their life is clearly higher priority.

9 **Lie behind them** and prone paddle to safety.

If they're heavier than you it will take a determined effort. If they're very much heavier, you may have to call the Coastguard on 112 from a mobile phone anywhere in the world. Safety will be discussed later.

*Checking on the towee can give a beast of burden a break!*

The rescue procedure.

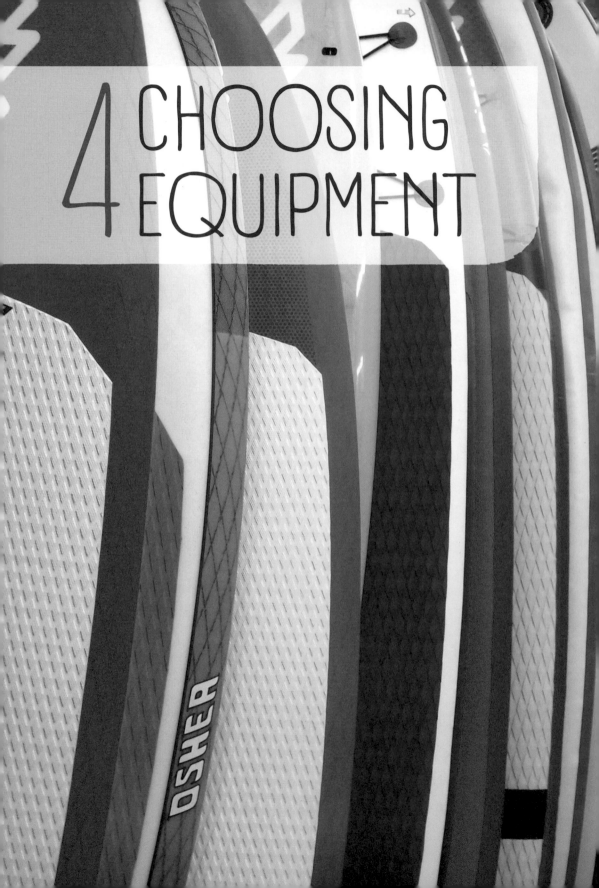

# 4 CHOOSING EQUIPMENT

Once you've tried, or at least considered, different SUP activities (tours, surf, yoga, races, etc.) you'll be ready to think about whether to buy equipment and clothing. This will give you the flexibility to paddle when and where you want without paying for hire, be it a half-hour blast or a weekend away. The following information will help you choose what to purchase.

# Boards

Buying a paddleboard is possibly more exciting than the first time you stand up on one, though it will normally involve more thought.

Becoming well equipped is no flipping flippant quipping matter but, after forking out the initial painful payments, ours can be a very cheap pastime. A good purchase, well looked after, could last for many years with no need to upgrade for each fleeting fad.

Take as many opportunities as you can to try a range of boards and SUP activities, when it's safe and within your capabilities. Many retailers and manufacturers (SUPpliers?) attend events, some called demo days, and most will let you try before you buy, or rent before you've spent. To some extent, if a board doesn't feel wonderfully stable at first, your balance may develop as you become used to it.

Initial considerations before buying your exciting new purchase may be:

- What activities am I likely to be doing and how often? This could be playing on the beach, touring the coast or inland, racing and/or surfing. If you want variety or you're unsure, an all-round multi-purpose board is a good choice.
- What can I transport and store? This may determine what sort of board, particularly rigid or inflatable, you choose.
- Is it just for you?
- What size board will suit me? We'll look into this.
- What's my budget?

Boards at H2O Watersports.

Events provide opportunities to try boards and other equipment. Some of them want to be used by you!

# High street or high spec?

You may not have much choice whether to paddle business or economy class. That said, there is a third option: second-hand, which may bring quality equipment within your grasp.

If purchasing new, here are some of the likely relative advantages of buying big or small budget kit:

## Cheaper (under £400):
- You may be able to afford two boards.
- Once you can upgrade, you'll have a useful spare.
- Less likely to be stolen.
- You may feel more at ease when lending to friends.
- Enables people of limited means to SUP.
- Helps keep down the price of other boards.

*Paddle rack.*

## Expensive (over £600):
- Better construction and more robust.
- More reliable for longer trips.
- Better balanced and efficient, so improved performance.
- Easier to keep up with friends.
- More specialist advice available.
- Paddle will be lighter and less of a strain.
- Helps companies that pioneer improvements.

Of course there are a whole range of prices with some mid-range (£400 to £600) boards available, often of good quality, particularly online, such as Sandbanks Style, though you may not be able to try them out. A trawl of the internet will catch a wide range of products and reviews. It will be interesting to see whether and how much prices come down generally with greater availability of more affordable makes of boards counteracting the effects of inflation (especially with blow-up ones!).

If you have a budget of £800 for your paddle and board, how will you divide it between them? We'll come to paddle options, but don't go too cheap on the paddle. A slightly heavier paddle will give you a good workout but won't be efficient. A very cheap paddle with a metal shaft with no flexibility could leave you with lasting shoulder problems. So you may want to allow at least £85 for the paddle. There are some good deals, particularly online.

Bear in mind if you divide your budget into paddle £200 and board £600, compared to £100/£700, you'll have a paddle twice as good, probably made with light carbon fibre, and a board that's around 85% as good. This is a better balance, though you could take it too far. It's cheaper to upgrade your paddle later on than your board. A spare is also useful, particularly if one of them divides up for ease of transport. Many deals include a paddle and pump with inflatable boards, which can be more cost effective, though only if they give the kind of quality/performance you would like. They may let you upgrade the paddle for an advantageous price.

Boards in bags.

Jon Popkiss, Director of Kai Sports in Southampton, uses the analogy that if the board is like a car, you are the engine and the paddle is the transmission. A great board won't perform well without a good paddle.

Some cheap boards can feel very disappointing compared to good makes in terms of stability, steering, performance and the quality of the fittings. With inflatables, if it doesn't inflate to at least 14 psi, it's a glorified li-lo. With less well-made SUPs there is more likelihood of a serious problem while out on a tour, especially if you're alone.

If you seek second-hand boards, you won't necessarily have many choices but there are boards available on social media sites, mentioned in the forums section (see page 241). As with most previously owned things you need to do research. Why are they selling? What's the condition? Make sure the valve works on inflatables. What would it cost new?

Bearing in mind you probably won't get any kind of warranty, some people seem to ask a lot for used boards. That said it may be worth a punt (pardon the 'punty' pun).

Another way is to look around the watersports schools and hire companies in September or October. Their kit will have had a lot of use, so obviously check the condition, but you may get a very affordable offer, especially if they know you.

# Rigid or inflatable

One of the main choices is whether to go for rigid or inflatable (sometimes referred to as ISUPs or inflatos). Your capacity to store and transport your board will influence this. However, your priorities may change. You may decide to buy a roof rack, though life changes may mean your spare room could be needed for other things.

Tez Plavenieks, founding Editor of SUP Mag UK, says inflatables accounted for around 80% of board sales in the UK and

the lion's share across Europe, though not necessarily worldwide, based on 2018 data. He believes the inflatables share has continued to increase since then.

Rigid boards are usually made in the same way as surfboards, with a piece of shaped foam wrapped in layers of fibreglass and epoxy resin. Construction varies and some are stronger and lighter than others, but more expensive. Some include a layer of wood veneer for added strength. There are also moulded plastic boards, which are very durable and a little cheaper. They are, however, significantly heavier so not great for carrying or loading on roof racks, as well as being less responsive.

Here are some of the relative merits:

### Rigid:
● No pumping required, so more time and energy for paddling.
● Less affected by wind.
● More specialist shape, e.g. for racing or surf.
● Better performance.

### Inflatable:
● Generally slightly cheaper, depending on quality.
● Less painful to land on or when it whacks your shins, or anyone else.
● Less easily damaged (spot the 'dink' in the photo).
● Lighter.
● Easier and safer to transport (no roof rack and straps required).
● Less easy to steal if inside your car.
● Easier to store.
● Easier to fly with.
● Gives you a warm-up if you hand pump ...
● So you'll never have 'chicken' or 'bingo wings'.

Inflatables often come in a neat rucksack-style bag. The leading makes in the UK include Red Paddle Company and Fanatic, though there are several other respected brands. Red are based in south west England and John Hibbard, who founded the company, is credited with having the idea of developing inflatable boards back in 2008.

## ISUP CONSTRUCTION

**PVC with woven inner:** Outer skin strength is important for long life and pressure capacity.

**Comfortable grippy deckpad:** The best deck pads are machine pressed in addition to gluing.

**UV resistant:** Built to withstand long-term exposure to sunlight, minimising material decay and keeping colours clear and vibrant.

**Fusion technology:** An additonal layer of PVC is laminated to the dropstitch core. Fusion results in a lighter, stiffer, longer lasting board, and it's much better for the environment than toxic glues.

**Triple layer on rail:** A 3rd and final layer around the rail of the board creates a second seal and ensures there are no weak points on the board.

**Super reinforced, high density dropstitch:** The strength/lightness ratio of the fibres is key to creating a super rigid but light board.

**Heat treated seal:** A laminated, heat pressed inner seam of the fused PVC surrounding the core of the board creates a 100% airtight and waterproof seal. Much better and stronger than gluing.

ISUP construction is sometimes referred to as 'dropstitch technology'. Essentially a thousand or more internal threads hold the top and bottom layers together in a rigid shape, once fully inflated. Some boards are described as single-skinned and others are double, which makes them slightly heavier, more robust, slightly slower but less affected by wind. Double-skinned feel stronger when deflated. Some have more strengthening features than others, such as an extra PVC layer along the centre line from nose to tail, known as a 'stringer', on both top and base.

Well-made boards are very tough. I own an early inflatable, now regarded as an antique by SUP standards, but it has stood the test of time. Red Paddle Company have made videos of their

*Whitesands Bay, Pembrokeshire. Five minutes faffing, then you're laughing.*

## GO GREEN

Some companies such as Starboard, another of the watersport world's leading names, are working to make the construction of both ISUPs and rigid boards more sustainable. Natural materials like pine and flax, bioresins and recycled plastic are incorporated.

inflated ISUPs surviving a tractor riding over one. They smeared another with dog food to see whether it would survive labradors, which they termed a 'lab test'. This may be another source of nearly new tested boards! I don't know whether they've tried sharks yet.

Some people really struggle with pumping up, but there are more efficient pumps, albeit more expensive. You can also purchase an electric pump that works from a car cigarette lighter. A reasonable battery can fill an average board, without a problem, to the prescribed pressure. Some can be used to fully deflate boards too. For more than one board or a large board you may have to leave your engine running. This can make the air around you somewhat unhealthy, particularly for friends or others using hand pumps. Try to park downwind of them or they may think you're looking smug through the smog.

The nozzles on some electric pumps are notorious for pressing on the valve as you remove them, with a loss of pressure, so you may find hand pumps less frustrating or worth taking too. If you're lucky enough to live near water and have the storage, ISUPs can be left inflated and checked from time to time.

*When deflating, warn people nearby of the sudden noise and beware the blast of air!*

# Board design

Boards vary in design particularly to specialise in touring, racing or surfing. As mentioned, if you aren't intending to stick mainly to a specific activity, or you aren't sure, then your board, or first board, should be an all-purpose design. These tend to be from 9ft 6in to 11ft 6in long and 30 to 32in wide with a rounded front end (nose). Most are around 10ft 6in. However, if you weigh around 14 stone/90kg or more you'll want something bigger. (Imperial measurements are more often given. The jargon is to say a 'ten six' for a 10ft 6in board.)

The more volume, the more stability, though the width is particularly important. An incredibly long but very narrow board would be very unstable. A slightly wider board will really help. Larger boards are less manoeuvrable and inflatables take more pumping, though if you are blessed with a bit more heft and strength than average it should help with this. There are particularly deep boards which don't tend to perform particularly well but are very stable and good if you want to take passengers. You can also add back rests to some boards, a bit like those for sit-on-top kayaks.

If you weigh around 8 stone/50kg or less, there is good news. You will probably be fine on one of the smaller all-purpose boards, which may be slightly cheaper as well as easier to steer and pump. A board that is too large could be difficult to control if windy. To some extent it depends on your balance, and information is no substitute for giving a board a good try to see how you feel on it. Bear in mind the quality of the paddle could affect this too (see page 58).

Red have now developed a 9ft 6in board that folds in half lengthways before you roll it up around a pump. By fitting into a more compact bag it makes carrying, particularly on public transport or on foot, much easier. The most compact packages come with five-piece paddles and there's even a board designed to be taken on a plane as hand luggage, the Aquaplanet Stowaway SUP. Some boards come in 'wheelable' bags. A design that could be trailed behind a bicycle would be handy and environmentally friendly, though boards may fit in conventional cycle trailers.

Some ISUPs state their volume in litres. To give you a guide as to how many litres of board you need, multiply your weight in kilograms by 3. So a 60kg paddler would want a board of around 180 litres, a little less would be fine with good balance. If your weight in kg is more than the board volume in litres you would sink! Boards tend to be 5 or more often 6in thick these days. Boards with a depth of 4in were found to lack the necessary stiffness, as well as being less buoyant. A rough guide to a suitable width would be:

| Weight in kg | Width in inches |
| --- | --- |
| <50 (8 stone) | 28 |
| 60 | 30 |
| 80 | 32 |
| 100 | 34 |

Having a board with mesh or stretchy strings (shock cord) attached to keep dry-bags and other items secure is an advantage. These can be fitted to ISUPs if they don't come with them, though you

*If you've shoulders like boulders, which might frighten a Titan, you'll need a broader board!*

can attach a dry-bag to the front end of your handle without much inconvenience if you're touring. Chandlers sell the cord quite cheaply. A board bag that folds up small so it can fit in a dry-bag or in the mesh with your pump may be useful on some paddle expeditions.

Boards also need a carry handle. Some early rigid boards lacked this, which made them very difficult to carry. Now most have a slot in the middle, or offset to one side to better suit arm length. Alternatively, some have a handle you can slide/pull out. ISUPs have an attached central handle, sometimes padded for comfort. Some kayaks have small wheels like a suitcase, though I've not seen SUPs with these yet. If you live 10 minutes from water, there are trolley arrangements and some SUP bags have wheels.

SUPs can combine to make a colourful scene. Performance aside, one small advantage of buying a brand new board is they often look great with distinctive colours. These have tended to fade a little, particularly the stick-on traction decks (the grippy bit) so red may end up pink here, though many are now UV resistant.

As a wildlife enthusiast, I was drawn to the lush leafy design of Sandbanks Style's 'Amazon' board. I've not had a kingfisher land on its camouflaged deck, but I've had some particularly good views of them from it. Perhaps a water-coloured board with some reflective qualities would blend in well and enhance the feeling of walking on water?

On some boards the deck grip curves up at the back, known as a 'kicker', which can be helpful when performing step back

Deck grip with raised back.

turns or manoeuvres in the surf stance. There are a multitude of minor individual design features that can make a difference. For instance, some ISUPs have strips or battens that you fit in the rails to give extra protection and rigidity. Whether this merits the extra preparation time, like other design features, is a matter of personal preference.

You may see particularly large ISUPs (megaSups) for groups. There are also boards of around 15ft long and a little wider for two people to ride on or much wider (around 5ft) boards for families.

Another design feature on some boards, known as wind Sups, allows them to be converted into windsurf boards, enabling you to transfer your balance skills and make the most of days when it's too windy to paddle. There are

inflatable windsurf rigs, which are easier to transport and less likely to cause injury, along with attachable fin arrangements known as 'drift-stoppers'.

Perhaps the most futuristic way to enjoy the sport is to have a foil underneath your board, enabling those seeking more of an adrenaline rush to ride above the water at considerable speed. The board is supported above a shaft connecting it to a specially designed winged fin arrangement (the foil) underneath. Boards need to be

MegaSups require team work.

MegaSups also need a mega parking space.

Foil under a windsurf board.

foil-compatible to attach one and, being new and specialised, tend to be expensive. This phenomenon has only got off the ground (or water!) since 2017 but is growing fast.

When they pick up speed, they can go much faster than a conventional SUP as the board itself rises higher than the water surface with less resistance. A pumping action, leaning back and forth, is used to lift the boards above the water. With speed comes added risk of injury to you and others, though they are an exciting option on days with a bit more

wind and can also be used in surf or behind a boat. Foils are being applied to various watersports. They enable kite-surfers to ride on days when the wind is less strong, which could increase risks to Suppers.

Supping above the surface has taken off in Southern California.

# Maintenance

Rinsing your equipment with cold water and allowing it to dry will extend its life, as well as help with biosecurity. Very mucky boards, perhaps after an estuary paddle, can be sprayed with ecofriendly SUP Scrub and wiped clean, though the deck grip may need brushing. Rigid boards can also be waxed for grip if they lack a stick-on grip. Check the condition of your equipment after use. Punctures to inflatables are rare, though they can happen. I took a board to Ireland on the ferry, with plans to head out across Lough Swilly. Perhaps fortunately, my first outing was on a canal and as I walked around a lock I heard a slight hissing sound. Sadly it wasn't just a swan and I found a tiny puncture, possibly from a thorn. It was a second-hand, single-skinned board from a watersport provider, so it had seen much active service.

ISUPs sometimes come with a puncture repair kit, with patches that can be cut to size, but the glue tends to dry up after the first use. The area should be cleaned, dried and lightly sanded first, as you would with a bicycle inner tube. I put a larger second patch over the first small one with an all-purpose, not water-soluble, glue which has been OK, though I probably won't be crossing the Irish Sea again with that board and definitely not on it. Professional repairers can do a very good job if you prefer to leave it to someone else.

Decathlon stock repair kits with 'high-pressure resistant MEK glue', which could also be useful if your deck grip comes away. Other sources are available, particularly online. If air leaks from the

*Repair kit with valve key.*

valve, a small turn with a valve key may solve the problem; these tend to have six or eight cogs. The only other serious problems I've heard of were a board being pumped mechanically to too high a pressure (a blow-up SUP?) and a cheap inflatable on a sunny day where the air inside expanded - more bang for your buck!

With rigid boards cracks or dings can occur when removing boards from roof racks, as well as from hitting other boards, rocks or groynes. Prevention could be preferable to cure, and transparent, low-friction rail tape can be used to protect the sides of boards. The good news is that small problems can be easily mended yourself. Firstly dry the

*A battered board can be restored!*

*Sand thoroughly; leave no flakes unsmoothed.*

*Fibreglass patch with epoxy above and below.*

board out. A short-term solution can be effected using gaffer tape or super glue to seal the area. There are also various repair kits, consisting of epoxy glue and rapid repair putty.

A better outcome can be achieved if you have more time. After drying the board, sand the affected area thoroughly with 120 grit sandpaper or a sander. Any holes can be filled with a mixture of epoxy resin and fibreglass filler. Once sanded, rub on epoxy, place a fibreglass patch over this and secure with more epoxy. Once dry, sand this down with 240 grit sandpaper or a sander. This can then be

sprayed with car spray paint. Don't use polyester on an epoxy board.

A specialist repairer can restore small problems to perfect condition for £40–100 and even fix major damage for £200 or less.

# Paddles

Paddles come in different designs. One important factor is that they should have some flexibility in the shaft. If not they will put a lot of strain on your shoulders, which can lead to problems, particularly in the muscles of your rotator cuffs. The pain will often be felt on the front side of your shoulders, though with physiotherapy, good posture and a flexible paddle you should solve the problem.

Try holding a potential purchase with the blade touching the floor a stride length in front of you. If you push down toward you, there should be some flex, with the middle of the shaft moving a little (1 or 2 cm) toward you. A good shop will know this, though hopefully it won't snap! Too much flex will be inefficient.

Some paddles are adjustable in length, which is very useful if you're going to do different activities, if you're squatting more going upwind or in waves, or if other people might use them. Some adjust to shorter lengths than others. There are two main types of mechanism. One involves pushing the sides of the mechanism back with your thumbs, lining up a hole around the required length and pushing back in, being careful not to pinch the skin on your hands. These can become stiff, particularly due to sand and saltwater, so rinse after use. If they are badly stuck, warm water may help.

The other type, which is more common on expensive paddles, involves pulling a clip back, adjusting to any length, then pressing the clip back over. One problem that can occur, especially if the clip has only one nut (some have two), is that sand wears the shaft a little thinner just where you normally have the clip. This means the clip can work loose. They can be tightened with a screwdriver or Allen key, though eventually they may need a little tape to thicken them. If they work loose on a paddle it can be very frustrating, so you may want to add a tool to your dry-bag list. Some single nut ones can be tightened by rotating the clasp around.

Adjustable paddles can still be a little long for the shorter Supper. The leading brands also produce paddles for children.

Many paddles can be separated into two or three pieces, which is very handy for travelling. They can fit in an ISUP bag. It can affect the flexibility of the shaft and they need rinsing to keep the clip in good order. If your hands are cold it can be difficult to separate them. If the metal stud becomes hard to push in, carefully using a ballpoint pen with a pointy lid can help, as can lubrication.

For the dedicated racer or other discipline specialist, non-adjustable, single-piece paddles are the lightest, most efficient option. Racers cut these to

the required length, making sure they don't cut too short, and use epoxy glue to secure the handle. Some racers hold the paddle below the handle when going into the wind as an alternative to shortening the shaft. Race paddles may have a little less flex.

Various materials and combinations of them are used to make SUP paddles, mainly the following:

● **Carbon fibre** – generally regarded as the best. They are the most expensive, often over £160, but they are the lightest (around 600–650g). For touring and racing this makes them more efficient and easier on the muscles. Cheaper ones have become available online.

● **Fibreglass** – more affordable, though usually over £100. They are quite light (950–1000g), but noticeably heavier and harder work than the above. They do tend to be more durable and have slightly more flex, so if you're not planning to do

*With a metal shaft the only flexibility is in the plastic blade.*

races or many long trips they're a good option. Many paddles combine some glass with carbon, with some advantages of both, for instance a carbon shaft and glass blade.

● **Pine** – individual and beautiful, and strong if well made. Weight wise they are in between the two previous (750–800g), though with pine proportionally more of the weight will be in the blade, which will make them seem slightly heavier. The main drawback is that they will not be adjustable.

● **Metal (aluminium alloy)** – heavy (around 1.1kg) and not enough flex, though some comes from having a plastic polymer blade. They don't all float, though some have foam in to keep them buoyant. I have seen the bottom section of one become detached on a tour and sink before anyone nearby could grab it. Some are padded, otherwise the shaft can feel cold in the lower hand.

● **Bamboo** is combined with carbon fibre on some paddles, making them stronger but a little heavier. This versatile natural material has been used to make rafts and paddles since time immemorial. Being strong, light and buoyant it is also used in some boards.

Handles are often a rounded T-shape or triangular, and there are chunkier varieties that may suit those with large hands. It's a matter of preference. The shafts are either round or oval. More expensive paddles tend to be oval, which may allow better grip and keeps the handle perfectly aligned with the blade on adjustable models with clip release. It also gives more strength in the direction force is applied.

All blades should be angled away from the paddler for technique reasons mentioned, though there is some variety in size and shape:

● **Flat blades** provide good power and are probably the most efficient.
● **Scooped blades** are curved (viewed from the side) to grab the water well at the start of the stroke, but are inefficient when lifted from the water. This is a feature of some plastic blades.
● **Dihedral blades** (when viewed from the far/bottom edge) have two slight curves either side of a spine down the centre. They are designed to prevent the blade from 'fluttering' (waggling slightly) as you bring it back. The side nearest you (the back of the blade or power face) resembles the underside of a moth with its wings folded down, so it is ironic that it stops fluttering, but if you have that tendency it should help. They also are

Natural design for paddle blades of the future?

less efficient to lift from the water. Whereas beaver tails resemble flat blades, a swan's feet are a little like dihedral blades, with three main toes, one at each side and one in the middle. They splay them out for the power phase and bring the toes together for their recovery phase.

Bigger blades, which are sometimes more rounded like a tear drop, may suit stronger paddlers when touring or racing. They provide more power but are harder work, tough on the shoulders and not so good for acceleration and cadence (rate of paddling). If you are mightier than most, possibly someone who prefers to cycle in a higher gear than average, they may be for you. As SUP has developed, blades have tended to become smaller as higher cadence is thought to be preferable to using more power. Surfers and white water paddlers tend to prefer the more responsive blades with less surface area for bursts of acceleration, though the blade is also useful for support strokes, so very powerful surfers may prefer broader blades.

Some companies, like Chinook, specialise in paddles. Manufacturers often feature their logos on the front of the blade. They don't seem to label blades 'front'

Generally blade size has reduced.

and 'back', but it could help beginners! Instructors would have far less reason to justify their role, so maybe I'm glad.

Like boards, it's good to rinse after use. To help keep your paddle as good as new, you can fit a length of protective rubber around the edge of your blade. This is a good idea if you paddle in shallow rivers. Some glues are water-soluble so use one that isn't and allow it to set properly. The rubber strip will make the paddle slightly less efficient. Retailers will sometimes spare you enough for free.

Blade protection can prevent chips and splits.

# Pumps

One of the most important things to remember with inflatable boards is to have the valve in the outermost position when inflating.

You have to push it in and twist to let the air out, but it's probably wise to then leave it outward ready for its next inflation

Pump with two chambers.

to avoid the frustration and exhaustion of it deflating as soon as you remove the pump.

Manual pumps have improved in recent years and there are several types. These include large single chamber high volume pumps, though with these alone it is very hard to achieve enough pressure. There are slimmer higher pressure varieties, which are slower, though starting with the former and finishing off with the latter works well. Another variety, though almost twice as expensive, inflates on the pull stroke as well as when pushing down. This is generally a lot faster and easier and warms up more muscles, though people with back issues sometimes find the greater resistance when pulling up a concern. Bending your knees to use your legs helps. Pumps should have a pressure gauge.

Many people regard the best pumps to be those with two chambers, which can be switched from very high volume to high pressure. However, these can be three or four times the price of a basic model. Some pumps have three settings that you can easily switch between:

1 **Inflate as you push** and pull until pulling becomes hard.

2 **Inflate further** with high volume just on the push down.

3 **Finish off** with high pressure and less volume.

Decathlon sell a cheaper version (around £75) with the Itiwit brand. Make sure the pump and hose are threaded together correctly.

Pumps can get a little clogged up inside after much use. It is worth carefully taking them apart occasionally, removing any build-up of dirt and spraying the moving parts with lubricant to keep them efficient.

# Leashes

A strong breeze or the flow of a river can move your board faster than swimming pace. So you don't lose your beautiful new board and the safety it brings, a leash is an essential purchase, and shouldn't cost much. They are strong and slightly stretchy with Velcro loops at each end to attach to you and your board. One lady I taught thought one might be useful for taking her husband shopping! The two main types are:

● **Uncoiled** – good for surfing, but not great for touring and racing as they can drag in the water and snag on waterweed and flotsam. If other Suppers' blades catch them you'll do well to remain high and dry. For surfing they should be as long as or slightly longer than your board so you fall away from them, though for touring shorter ones reduce the chance of snagging. Leashes vary, but tend to be around 7mm thick. The extra demands surfing places on them means a stronger, thicker one would be better for surfing.

● **Coiled** – alleviates the problems above so are better for tours and races but can

*Some wear a coiled leash high on the calf, so it's less likely to be trodden on or tripped over.*

Leash attached to waist belt.

feel slightly restrictive if too short for a long board and may impede surfers.

The leash is usually secured to the paddler's ankle; some prefer the top of their calf, so they are less likely to tread on it. The latter needs to be tight or it will slip down anyway, though some are designed to fit here. The other option, with either kind, is to attach them to a quick release waist belt. These are much safer for white water or fast rivers and can be undone by pulling a toggle at the front. Flight attendants are the best qualified people to demonstrate this!

A buoyancy aid is one of your best friends.

# Buoyancy aids

An essential purchase is a buoyancy aid, also known as a personal floatation device. In Europe these should be CE tested and approved. CE will be printed on the inside. (Type III are normally worn in the US.) These will help you float, stay warm and may prevent injury. They should fit fairly snugly with adjustable straps to avoid riding up. It's important that they should be an effective aid to staying afloat. A larger individual will require more buoyancy. However, they must be comfortable and allow a full range of movement, as well as breathing, or it would defeat the object. Although they come in different sizes, the straps help them to fit different body shapes. They don't tend to be gender specific. There are a range of very sleek and stylish options, though Decathlon sell very affordable ones. I bought one with pockets for non-bulky items. A small water bottle and water-proof camera don't seem to impede paddling motion. The foam can deteriorate so it is worth replacing them every three years.

'What do we like best about SUP?'
'She has to wear the leash for a change.'

# Clothing

Walk into a good watersports retailer and you will see an array of racks with all manner of items to prepare you for paddling. The staff will be able to explain the various options. Some will also have informative websites. The choice comes down to:

● What activities will you be doing?
● What temperatures will you be doing them in?
● Your budget.
● Personal preference and comfort.
● How likely you are to wobble.

If you're SUP surfing for any length of time in the UK, you'll want a wetsuit, but for touring there are several options depending on the temperatures of the air and water and how likely you are to tumble:

● **Swim kit** – fine on a warm day.
● **Running kit** – wickable and quick drying, though you can take a spare dry top. They often give UV protection as well.
● **Water resistant tops** or 'technical clothing', like a smart T-shirt, are very quick drying and don't restrict movement but can be expensive. Can be muted colours if you hope to see wildlife, or bright to 'be seen, be safe'.
● **Thin neoprene tops** and/or leggings – if you get wet they warm up a little layer of water underneath.

● **Neoprene jackets** – not cheap but good for a range of temperatures as can be worn zipped, unzipped or easily removed. Great for instructors between sessions.
● **Gloves** – flexible water-resistant gloves with good grip are a blessing on cold day tours. Divers' neoprene gloves tend to be hard to grip with.

Wetsuit racks in retailer H2O.

● **Wetsuits** – various designs described below, can be worn over swim or running kit or 'rash vests', which are normally made of lycra and prevent chafing, especially on your neck.
● **Boots, gloves, hats and hoods** – described below. Helmets will be mentioned in the whitewater and surf chapters.
● **Water shoes** may be useful in summer if you have a fair walk, especially over uncomfortable surfaces.
● **Dry-suits** – unlike many wetsuits these aim to keep you dry. They're bulky and warm so only worth wearing if the weather is very cold or the water is and there's a fair chance you'll be in it, for instance in white water (see page 206).

4 · CHOOSING EQUIPMENT

*Technical tops.*

## Neoprene

This form of rubber clothing was developed in the 1940s and '50s. It has played a crucial part in the evolution of some watersports such as surfing. It tends to be nylon-lined to ease on and off. It can also have some nylon-lining on the outside for increased durability.

Hoods are more of a feature for divers, though separate neoprene hoods or hats with chin-straps can be useful for paddling or surfing on crisp winter days. A woolly hat, possibly plus a spare in your dry-bag, is a good option for chilly tours, though neoprene is better if you're likely to tumble. Neoprene boots can be pretty much essential for Supping in colder months, though they do reduce your feel for the board. A few hardy surfers tough it out in bare feet for this reason, though having had frostbite in a couple of toes (not through watersports) I prefer to stop my feet getting ridiculously cold as chilblains can be extremely uncomfortable.

Some boots have separate compartments for your big toes which give more grip and stop your feet from rolling in them. Others have separate compartments for each toe, which look somewhat tree frog-like, and aren't quite as warm, but would give good grip. Suppers don't tend to use these. Some boots only come to the top of your ankles and have small holes to let water in and out, so you don't end up with lots of water in them. These are good in the sea or rivers when the water isn't very cold. Some come a little higher up. The thickness tends to be between 2mm and 5mm, but obviously it's a compromise between warmth and feel for the board. The feet have thicker neoprene than the ankles on some. There are also neoprene socks, which give less protection from cold or from stones on the shore. In urban rivers some form of footwear is always advisable. Foot injuries are a risk near structures, such as bridges, on all rivers.

Wetsuits have continued to improve over the decades. They come in various types including:

● **Vest style shoulders or 'long john'** – allow full shoulder mobility and easy to get on; useful if water is warm but breeze is cool, though you can get quite cold if you fall in.
● **'Shortie'** – short arms and legs – keeps your body warm but allows more flexibility than a full wetsuit.

• **Full wetsuit or 'steamer'** – these come in different thicknesses to cope with different temperatures. Winter ones tend to be 5mm on the body and 4mm on the limbs, whereas others may be 3mm and 2mm, respectively.

The inner, sponge-like layer warms up when wet, providing insulation. Wetsuits can make you feel quite hot, though the tops can be peeled down and the arms tied behind or in front of your waist. Older and cheaper wetsuits do tend to restrict your movement quite a lot. Some modern wetsuits have such good seams that, if you have a well-fitting one, keep your body dry and seal in warm air.

Wetsuits can get somewhat sweaty inside. By rinsing your wetsuit inside and out in cold water and allowing it to dry, ideally not in sunlight and not on direct heat such as a radiator, you will extend its life and help to keep its flexibility. Salty water isn't great for wetsuits and, given they can be expensive, it's worth looking after them. Soaking in warm (not hot) water before rinsing in cold helps. If you don't manage to rinse and dry them the aroma can be particularly unpleasant, though there are cleaning and conditioning products available. If neglected, even the most avid Supper or surfer wouldn't claim to love the smell of neoprene in the morning.

Traditionally wetsuits have a zip at the back with a cord for pulling up, or down to take off. Generally this makes them the easiest to peel down to cool off or lower a little to loosen the neck. Sometimes the cord can be hard to reach or may get caught in the wetsuit or the Velcro on the neck cuff. This can mean you have to approach a complete stranger and ask them for help with your zip.

Just when you thought your budget had taken all the big hits, it may be worth purchasing a comfortable modern wetsuit. They often cost over £100, typically well over for winter ones, but specialist retailers will sometimes sell off models from previous years at trade prices. They have more freedom of movement, termed 'four way stretch', and tend to look better or at least snugger. It's best to try them on to check you can breathe and have a good range of movement, particularly for SUP strokes.

More flexible wetsuits don't need to have the zip at the back. Some have zips across the upper chest or shoulders; others are zip-less, particularly semi-dry ones. These options tend to be harder work to get in and out of, particularly thicker winter ones. At least you won't have a zip you can't reach, so you probably won't look like you need help dressing or undressing.

*If wetsuits become too warm, the arms can be tied around your waist.*

# 5 PLACES TO GO, WILDLIFE TO SEE

Once you've mastered the strokes, Supping makes many picturesque landscapes and seascapes accessible. You may even be blessed with a stunning skyscape. One of the great pleasures SUP brings for many people are the beautiful and fascinating environments that can be explored. These can be broadly divided into flowing, still and salty. Seeing people's eyes lit up by a close encounter with nature is a very heartwarming aspect of leading SUP safari tours. Some of our most iconic wildlife may be encountered.

Shoal of dace.

Paddlers on Canada's Lake Louise.

# Rivers

The fastest flow in a river is usually between the middle and the outside bend. You can test this with Pooh sticks! This is well worth bearing in mind on your paddles, especially when battling upstream. Lowland rivers alternate between fast flowing shallow 'riffle' sections on straighter stretches and deep pools on the outside of bends with eroding steep banks as the meanders become more pronounced. Sometimes the inside of bends will have beaches of deposited material such as shingle.

# River wildlife

While paddling back gently downstream on my local river, I heard something enter the water on the left-hand bank - then noticed a light brown otter was swimming along next to the right side my board just ahead of my feet. The otter swam at the

*Otter and eel — nature raw in tooth and claw.*

than on the sea, with nature all around you including many creatures, the sight of which can make your day. On a board you can have unrivalled views of both banks as well as the landscape beyond. Standing on the water surface can also afford you a particularly good view down into the water. In a clear, healthy river you may see more fish than an angler could dream of shaking a stick or rod at. Looking straight down from a SUP reflections interfere less, compared to looking diagonally from a canoe. Also if a fish is 10cm below the surface you'll only have to look through the sediment in 10cm of water, rather than around 14cm if looking at 45°.

same pace as me for around five seconds, seemingly out of curiosity or playfulness, before dipping slightly, releasing a characteristic swirl of bubbles from its fur and swimming under my board.

The more you see wildlife the easier it becomes to spot. As you 'get your eye in' your brain recognises the shape, movement and behaviour of particular species, so you can increase your chances in the otter spotter lottery!

Paddling rivers feels more intimate

Heading or free-wheeling downstream smoothly and quietly, when you hardly have to paddle, you'll tend to see more wildlife. If you can completely rest your paddle for a minute or so, but keep your

## TOP TIP

Paddling, or battling, upstream, try to avoid the faster flow between the middle of the channel and the outside of bends. Tuck into small bays or places where the banks or vegetation provide shelter from the current or a headwind. Reed beds on the river edge will create friction, helping to slow the flow alongside them.

*What is this life if, full of care, we have no time to stand and stare? (From Leisure by WH Davies.)*

senses primed, you may well be rewarded. Often the river will guide you down the best route; it seems to know the way and you can simply go with the flow. It's worth staying alert as the wind may have other ideas and can conspire with the vegetation to leave you flummoxed on the fringe of the flume.

If the wind is blowing the opposite way to the flow, it will help you paddle upstream. It will also carry your scent away as you silently return downstream. Some animals, including otters, rely firstly on smell, before hearing and sight so this is another way to boost the odds of witnessing them.

## FISH

Salmon and trout inhabit swift-flowing well-oxygenated water. In winter they excavate hollows in the gravel of clear rivers in which to breed and lay their eggs, so it is particularly important not to disturb these furrows, known as 'reds'. The beautiful grayling may also be seen in such stretches. They have particularly striking, long reddish dorsal fins which the males use to wrap around females in courtship.

Slightly slower moving water is obviously easier to paddle. One of the commoner larger fish found here is the chub, with dark top and tail fins.

> **TOP TIP**
> ..........................
> Banks erode more on the outside of bends so there is more likelihood of fallen trees and exposed roots which are potentially serious hazards mentioned in Chapter 9.

Its sizeable fleshy mouth and keen appetite gave rise to the word 'chubby'.

The most numerous fish is probably the minnow. This small handsome species, with a prominent lateral line and bands of darker colour with a few speckles or spots on top, has the dubious honour of being an important part of the food chain. Males develop white tubercles in the breeding season. If you look carefully at large shoals of small fish, particularly in the well-oxygenated shallows, they may turn out to be dace: a pretty silver fish with a concave curve to its dorsal fin, shown at the start of this chapter. If you dangle your toes for a few minutes they may give you a free pedicure as they eat at your feet. (I'll spare you the photo!)

## BIRDS

The most colourful beneficiary from small fish is the exotic-looking kingfisher. On quiet river reaches you may be blessed with several sightings as a Supper, though it may be the same bird moving to the end of its territory before looping back. Sometimes they fly close past you with their rapid wing-beats and fast, low, level flight path. Listen for their high-pitched whistle of a call. Many people have never seen one. You may be rewarded for the effort of paddling by spotting one perched, possibly on a reed akin to a reed warbler, or hovering, resembling a kestrel or tern, before dart-diving to catch an unfortunate fish. Kayakers tend to see the orange underside. Standing brings more of the electric blue of their backs into view.

Although they are beautifully coloured, their shape is somewhat less graceful than many birds, but this is for a reason. The nest is a tunnel excavated well above the usual water level in the earth of riverside cliffs. Other than the chamber for the chicks, it is so narrow that they have to shovel earth out backward with their feet and stocky, spade-shaped tails.

*Colourful kingfisher.*

They're shy and secretive, so don't stay near their nests for long or the youngsters will go hungry.

A good time to see them is late summer and autumn, when the slightly less brightly coloured youngsters are seeking out territories. They may fly right past you while concentrating on chasing each other off. Fish are always swallowed head first after a few whacks on the perch. Females have a red lower bill and accept romantic gifts of fish from the males during courtship. This may go some way to make up for them being called 'king...' and not 'queenfishers'!

There are many other birds that appreciate a good river. Look out for a small white heron with a dark bill, known as a little egret, which has only become a common sight in Britain in the last few decades. Like other herons it nests in colonies in trees and flies with its long legs held up behind it, which must take impressive core strength! The great white

*King and Queenfisher. 'How charming!'*

egret, with a yellow bill and of similar size to the common grey heron, is also starting to appear on our waterways.

One big, beautiful bird to treat with the utmost respect is the mute swan. On narrow rivers if they are protecting cygnets, try to give them and their nests a wide berth. The male, known as a 'cob', has a noticeably larger round bulge on top of its bill, known as (bird terminology alert) a 'basal knob'. Situated just above the nostrils it could be described as a 'nasal blob'.

'Mute swan' is a slight misnomer. Both genders can be aggressive, particularly the male. This could involve hissing and neck arching, chasing you off their territory or flying up close to you. Try to remain calm. You could try speaking softly to them (in 'Swanish'). I have found making little tweeting noises, similar to those made by the cygnets, seems to help, as does tuneful whistling.

Turn back if practical on very narrow

Little egret and otter: 'We search the same streams; we want the same things.'

stretches. Sadly too much disturbance can cause them to abandon their nests. Please don't be aggressive back. It's only natural for them to protect their young, though you may want to be ready to shield yourself with your paddle in a non-threatening way. Many are owned by the Crown, and it is a criminal offence to hurt them. Some swans are quite peaceful, even friendly, and once the cygnets are a bit older they calm down quite a lot.

Cob with large basal knob and cygnet.

## FLOWING FLOWERS

A wonderful array of colourful wild flowers and their reflections can brighten up a SUP trip. Here are a few of the classics:

**Water forget-me-nots** produce masses of tiny, slightly pink buds which open into the familiar small pale blue flowers. Fresh back from the Crusades, the first thing a romantic German knight wanted to do was take his true love for a riverside walk, while still wearing his impressive armour. He bent down to pick a bunch of the blue flowers, but tumbled into the water. He threw them to his sweetheart, calling to her 'Vergisz mein nicht!' before

Water forget-me-not.

he drowned. His memory lives on, partly thanks to Samuel Taylor Coleridge, who wrote a poem about the incident popularising the English translation as the name. The moral of the story is don't pick wild flowers, at least not with your heavy armour on. Many of us may have yelled something 'bluer' when falling in!

**Purple loosestrife.** This tall, striking purple perennial was only named that way because the leaves resemble those of the unrelated yellow loosestrife, which was tied around the necks of cattle to repel insects, hence its name. Paddling alongside banks of these beautiful purple spikes could help you to find peace with the world and feel less strife, earning it the name in its own right.

**Brooklime.** The buoyant slightly fleshy stems and leaves of this creeping plant with small lilac flowers enable pieces that break off to become established elsewhere. Scientific names can seem formidable, though this species has a memorable one: *Veronica beccabunga*. It is a type of speedwell, which are all in the genus Veronica. The species name is wonderfully descriptive as it bungs up becks.

Purple loosestrife.

Brooklime.

THE PADDLEBOARD BIBLE

**Arrowhead** produces attractive white flowers and leaves that vary in form, depending on their height in relation to the river depth. Those that don't make the surface look like broad blades of underwater grass; those that just reach it have a slightly rounded arrow-like shape, but those that rise above the surface have a three-pointed distinct arrowhead shape. It seems to decide their form in advance.

Arrowhead.

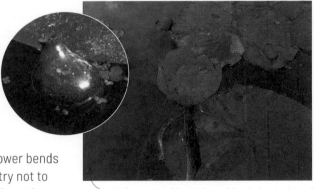

Yellow water lily (with seed head, inset picture).

**Yellow water lily.** These have characteristic large leaves held on buoyant stalks up to 3m long, rooted in the slower bends of rivers. They shelter fish, so try not to plough through them, especially as they can form a tough tangle around your fins. Some leaves remain near the bed and resemble lettuce leaves as you look down. The buttercup-yellow flowers smell of alcohol and become bulbous brandy bottle-shaped seed heads. Eating the stalks was thought to have, well, the opposite effect to oysters!

**Water crowfoot** is the classic tasseled plant that flows along rivers in great swathes just under the surface. These green manes harbour huge numbers of small fish and invertebrates. It is related to buttercups; the flowers are similar with yellow centres but white petals. The puzzle with this plant is how, in rivers that flow from the west with the prevailing wind, it ever colonises upstream. The crow's foot-shaped fronds have evolved to catch around the feet of water birds who tend to fly upriver, though most bits that break off will head toward the sea. The fins and leashes of paddleboarders could now be giving it a helping hand. Mind out, they get snarled in the thicker bits.

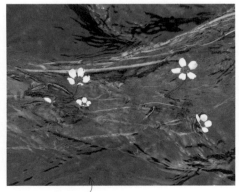
Water crowfoot.

*Dappled shade paddle.*

## TREES

Waterside trees help to give rivers an intimate feel and seasonal variation. They provide welcome dappled shade on hot days. When paddling into the wind, you can often tuck into the lea of trees on bends. They also add habitat interest including kingfisher perches and places for otters to shelter among their roots. Two types of tree are particularly adapted to life on the edge of water:

**Willow.** There are quite a few native species of willow which are great for wildlife, including some tough fast-growing examples such as Crack Willow which can lose large limbs and remain healthy while the logs that crack off re-root elsewhere.

The leaves contain salicylic acid which protects the tree from fungal infection and is the active ingredient in aspirin. The roots sometimes look pink under the water. They work together with bacteria that contain haemoglobin, the red protein that stores oxygen in our blood. This helps their roots to cope underwater.

*Weeping willows* Salix babylonica *were introduced from China in 1730. Weeping by rivers will forever be associated with Babylon thanks to Psalm 137 and Boney M.*

*Pink willow roots.*

**Alder** trees also love water and have similarly pink roots. Unlike willow trees, which are either male or female, alders produce catkins of both sexes on each tree. In winter the purple colouring of the many young male catkins gives the whole tree an attractive appearance. As the year moves on, the females swell and become rounded, while the males become floppy and droopy.

## A BROAD-TAILED BLAST FROM PAST

In the 1970s many rivers were 'canalised', removing all the pools, riffles and the backwaters that act as a nursery for fish fry and a shelter for much other wildlife, particularly when the flow is fast. Generally this didn't help with flood issues, whereas more natural features tend to even out fluctuations in the flow. Now many groups such as wildlife trusts, fishing groups and fish-related charities like the Wild Trout Trust are restoring the wildlife interest in rivers with angled staked logs and brushwood 'berms'. These resemble beaver dams along the riverside that recreate meanders and

provide a valuable wildlife refuge, particularly as they become vegetated.

While recently working for the Rivers Team of a wildlife trust, I was lucky enough to visit the Devon Beaver Project. These vegetarian mammals were an important part of the web of water life until man wiped them out in Britain a few hundred years ago. They don't build dams in large rivers so they won't inconvenience Suppers. They create ponds in boggy areas and small streams to provide enough depth for them to swim and build their lodges. They carry out a lot of habitat improvements and studies have shown that they improve water quality and benefit populations of fish and other native wildlife which had, after all, evolved to live with their activities.

Other beaver introductions have taken

Beavers have strong teeth and could carve a paddle if they didn't already have paddle-like tails.

place, or are planned, throughout Britain, including an established population in the Argyll region of Scotland.

While canoeing with my 'better half' in Western Canada a few years ago, we suddenly saw one right by the canoe, with a kit (youngster) held in its mouth. It slapped its tail a couple of times, which they do as a warning to keep away or even to splash you. We hadn't meant to disturb it, but it was wonderful to witness. The tail resembles a SUP blade. Many bright ideas come from nature!

The North American species is very slightly different to the European beaver, which has been successfully reintroduced in several countries and could be making a fascinating comeback in the UK.

*The conker-coloured blob is a wild Devon beaver.*

*The European beaver, with paddle-shaped tail.*

*On the Gloucester and Sharpness Canal, a warm welcome to Splatt, followed by a cooler one!*

# Canals

Towpaths along canals enable friends and families to walk, cycle and SUP together even when rivers are swollen and sea swells swirl. Calm canal waters can be good places for relatively new paddlers, though the wind can bring a wobble or fall, especially if you're tall and trying to learn a turn.

Canals can provide corridors for wildlife through industrial areas, and there are some surprisingly good urban venues for SUP. As well as canals, docks can provide striking backdrops. Some places wouldn't necessarily be safe to just roll up and unroll your board, but there are organised activities in cities such as Gloucester, Bristol and Liverpool, in Salford Quays and in London's Royal Victoria Dock.

Working as the ranger for a six-mile stretch of the Cromford Canal in Derbyshire, I became just as interested in the history as the natural history of these man-made waterways. Canals would have been busy bustling arteries of Britain in their heyday, complete with colourful characters and artwork often depicting roses and castles.

At the best access, there may be a small drop down to the water so you may have to put your far foot level with the handle and carefully mount your board in a squatting position while holding the bank. Look out for features like grooves in narrow bridges alongside towpaths worn away by the ropes from horses. You will probably come across (or rather under) swing bridges. Build up a little

*City slickers can unwind from the grind here in the dock.*

momentum, then be sure to get down low enough to go under safely by kneeling or lying and using small steering strokes or your hands.

Incredible feats of engineering, such as aqueducts, often feature and Supping is a great way to appreciate them and the views from them. You may also need to carry your board around locks. This may involve climbing metal ladders with narrow rungs, so neoprene boots, water

*Classic canal artwork.*

shoes or other footwear may make this less painful. Locks can also be found on navigable rivers. Canals were built to follow contours with locks to change altitude or sometimes tunnels to cope with tricky topography. Be particularly careful with these. Wear a head-torch or walk around for safety's sake.

*Feats of engineering include aqueducts like this at Limpley Stoke, near Bath.*

# Canal wildlife

While geographically canals may seem to appear like rivers, biologically they more closely resemble ponds. With straighter sides and more managed vegetation, they lack the varied flows and habitats of rivers, though they provide wonderful corridors for pond life unadapted to cope with faster flows. Although they generally follow contours, they can still take you on wonderfully scenic routes. The Caledonian Canal in Scotland is an awe inspiring expedition, while in Wales the Brecon and Monmouth Canal has some beautiful backdrops.

## MAMMALS

A favourite resident of canals is the water vole. On hearing a sudden plop from the bank, look out for this much-loved mammal swimming along or below the surface. Its tail is shorter than its body, unlike the less appealing rat. It also has a shorter nose and cuter rounded face by comparison. Sadly water vole populations have taken a dive in recent decades due to the spread of the American mink which predate on voles. Female mink will wipe out all the voles in their territory while bringing up young.

The Crinan Canal, near the Mull of Kintyre, Scotland.

American mink are smaller, darker and often bolder than otters.

Water vole.

Mink can be quite bold, but don't like too much disturbance. After I left, mink colonised the Cromford Canal from the nearby River Derwent while the towpath was closed in 2001 due to the foot and mouth outbreak. The recent success of otters is helping to control populations of mink, their darker, smaller invasive relative, which in turn is benefitting water voles.

On one occasion, while investigating a possible leak, I disturbed a water shrew. These localised, nocturnal mammals are rarely seen despite being over twice the weight of common shrews, but look out for their black bodies with white undersides, normally when disturbed.

The elusive water shrew.

# BIRDS

One of the most commonly seen birds on canals is the moorhen, with its red and yellow bill, not dissimilar to the coot, which has a white bill and white patch

Moorhen.

Coot.

extending up its forehead. The most fun to watch is the little grebe, also known as a dabchick, which dives under the water then appears a few seconds later several metres away.

## REPTILES AND AMPHIBIANS

The Cromford Canal is the only place in Derbyshire where people frequently spot grass snakes. It was exciting to see these proficient swimmers snake across the water or intertwine in courtship near a wide part of the canal designed for longboats to turn. Our longest British snake, they often grow to 90cm (3 feet) but females occasionally reach double that. It is quite eerie to see a snake that long in the UK, though they are harmless unless you're a small creature such as an amphibian. The humble frog is a target for so many predators from the moment it leaves the jelly-like sanctuary of the spawn.

## FISH

The most notable fish found in canals is the large-eyed, menacing pike, often seen lurking motionless among underwater vegetation. Youngsters, known as 'jack pike', have beautiful markings for camouflage. These vicious fish catch their prey, including other fish, more pitiable frogs and even water birds, using their long distinctive jaws lined with sharp teeth. Their sudden speedy movements are generated by their tails and their dorsal fins which are set far back close to the tail fin. Learning from nature, if you have a fin on your board that you can vary the position of, furthest back is fastest, though less far gives more manoeuvrability.

Another fish that appreciates the navvies' efforts is the predatory perch

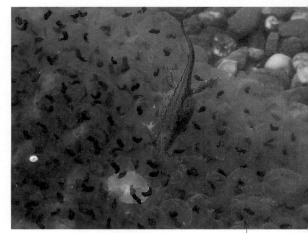

This newt can't wait for the tasty tadpoles to hatch.

Patterned young pike.

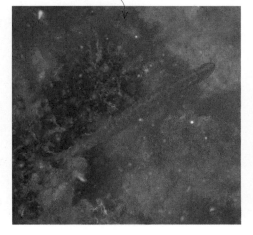

Tench and two perch. 'Why does every sick individual with a problem or parasite bring it to me?'

with its two tall distinctive dorsal fins and beautifully striped deep body. The rudd has aptly ruddy fins, a body which can range from metallic green to deep coppery brown and an upturned mouth for catching insects at the surface including midges and mosquitoes: a most welcome, much-appreciated choice!

The strong fins of the tench are designed to plough through the bottom mud. It also has a particularly thick layer of mucus to protect it from parasites that lurk in the murky depths. It was nicknamed the 'doctor fish' as it was believed sick fish would rub against it to benefit from some of its slimy protection. It is not often seen but females come up to the edge of the banks to spawn.

## FLOWERS

Canal-edge vegetation can be colourful and varied, thanks to banks and margins managed like meadows and flower seed wafted along by boats. Here are three to look out for:

Hemp agrimony.  Gypsywort.  Meadowsweet.

- **Hemp agrimony** has pink flowers which are favourite landing grounds for butterflies. The toothed leaves have a slight resemblance to another plant called hemp. Not particularly related to either, it is closer to the plant used for hemp rope than that of hemp 'dope'. The scientific name is *Eupatorium cannabinum*, though it is only the shape of the foliage that led to that kind of 'hash tag'.

- **Gypsywort** is another plant with toothed leaves. When it doesn't bare its small white flowers it could be easily confused with stinging nettle (this also grows on banks and has the appropriate scientific name: *Urtica dioica* – it 'urts!). However, the lighter green leaves of gypsywort have a different effect on the skin. It was made into an ointment used to darken skin by fortune tellers trying to look more authentic as Romanies, hence the name. Regular Suppers don't tend to need this traditional fake tan.

- **Meadowsweet** has red stalks and creamy frothy flowers, a little like the head on a good pint of ale. The flowers are actually used to flavour alcoholic drinks and the name is not derived from meadow but from mead, the fermented honey drink. The leaves, like willow, contain the active ingredient of aspirin. So it is possible to get enjoyably sozzled with the help of the flowers and then cure the following day's hangover using the leaves.

# Lakes

Lakes vary in size and character from large ponds to vast lakes such as Lough Neigh in Northern Ireland. No widely recognised definition exists for when a pond becomes a lake. They can range from deep upland lakes with low nutrients, fed by the high rainfall of mountainous areas and created by glacial processes, to shallow man-made, much vegetated lowland ones.

The larger and more exposed they are the more they will be affected by the weather and the higher their altitude the more weather they are likely to be subjected to. On a breezy day when local winds are throwing up high waves on the sea only suited to experienced SUP surfers, a large lake nearby, say over 0.5km wide, may have choppy waves less than half this height on the exposed side furthest from the oncoming wind.

Upland lakes can have wonderfully clear water.

Lake Geneva, Switzerland: lakes let you SUP amid spectacular scenery.

However, the sheltered side could be gently rippled and offer good possibilities for a paddle. We will consider the factors affecting waves more later. Remember not to start a trip with the wind behind you or you may struggle to return!

Small lakes can be very sheltered by trees or landscape. They are much less weather dependent and you can get to know them intimately if you live nearby. Many have been created as a by-product of extraction industries, such as gravel pits. Where there are several in an area there is a fair chance Supping will be allowed on one.

## Lake wildlife

Large bodies of water offer more possibilities for exploration and Supping is often allowed at least in some areas/ zones, though reservoirs are likely to have some restrictions. They may have large numbers of birds present, such as various species of ducks and geese valuing the open water, seeking safety in numbers and the opportunity to avoid human activity. As with all areas it is important not to cause too much disturbance.

Unlike the more uniform sides of a canal, lakes are likely to have a wider range of habitats. This may include islands which give a paddle a sense

Grasmere, Cumbria.

*Peel Island, Coniston Water, Cumbria, known as Wild Cat Island in Arthur Ransome's book Swallows and Amazons published in 1930.*

of adventure as in the book *Swallows and Amazons*. Islands can also provide a sanctuary for some of our wildlife from predators and people. Some may be private so look out for signs.

## VEGETATION

Boggy areas around the margins will support a range of plants including the beautiful and alliteratively named bog bean and marsh marigold, along with angelica which is cultivated so the green

*Bog bean.*

*Marsh marigold.*

*Water mint.*

*Reed warblers and cuckoo chick. 'Are you sure we're feeding it the right amount?'*

stalks can be candied for cake decoration. There is also a marsh mallow with prominent pink petals and roots that were used to flavour the confectionery with its name.

If you detect a pleasant smell while paddling, you may want to thank the wife of Pluto. The Greek god (not the Disney dog) developed a soft spot for the daughter of a river-keeper, a beautiful nymph named Minthe. Perhaps understandably, his possessive partner Persephone, goddess of vegetation, decided to nip this affair in the bud and turned her into the plant water mint. Minthe's appeal still shines through with perky pinky-purple flowers and aromatic culinary leaves. Scrunch one near your nose and sniff, in memory of mythical Minthe!

## BIRDS

Reed beds can provide wonderfully impenetrable hiding places for birds, though you may see marsh harriers hunting over them. If you're lucky, you could hear the resonant booming call of the secretive bittern, a large brown, well-camouflaged type of heron that holds its bill up to resemble a reed. They are rare, but fortunately the 'boom' can carry for miles to attract a mate.

You may also see or hear reed warblers which are only found among reeds. The similar sedge warbler has a white stripe above its eye and varies its habitat. The former has the unwanted honour of being the favourite surrogate parent for cuckoos, which are themselves now becoming rare.

The RSPB started up in 1889 as several bird protection issues were raising concern. The

*The camouflaged bittern is rare and protected, but listen for its boom.*

Banded demoiselle on water crowfoot.

Taming the dragon; common darter dragonfly.

passion for using feathers in fashion almost wiped out the great crested grebe. Thankfully this charity's efforts and the creation of many gravel and clay pit lakes has led to a very successful recovery. Grebes' spectacular courtship dancing displays involve presenting each other with gifts of pondweed.

The creatures that go through the most dramatic transformation as they emerge from water are the dragonflies. They generally spend two or three years as voracious predatory nymphs eating anything they can get their jaws into and jet propelling themselves by firing out air behind them. To be fair they are not the

Great crested grebes.

*Towing a tern raft.*

wing with their remarkable flying skills.

They may fly close to you as they patrol their territory. If you see one perched you can very slowly move your little finger in front of it and it may climb on so you can have a close look. When at rest they spread their wings out to the sides. The much slimmer damselflies close their wings behind them when settled. The largest two species of damselflies, called demoiselles, prefer rivers but many more species prefer the still water of canals, lakes and ponds.

most attractive of creatures, but at this stage they don't have to be. When they're ready, they crawl up emergent vegetation and force themselves out of their skins. After a few vulnerable hours pumping blood into their wings they become beautiful adult dragonflies for the next few weeks, able to colonise new ponds, attract a mate and catch other insects on the

There are two lakes on Brownsea Island in Poole Harbour, home to red squirrels. Although the island is mainly owned by the National Trust, the lakes

*Sandwich terns have black legs and a black bill with a yellow tip.*

are part of a nature reserve managed by Dorset Wildlife Trust. While working on a contract for their Reserves Team in 2016, we constructed three floating rafts to locate in the middle of the lakes for terns to nest on. These birds can often be seen in the harbour suddenly diving into the water like arrows to catch fish, sometimes just in front of your board.

As we lacked a boat, I leapt at the chance to bring a paddleboard to tow the rafts to the middle of the lakes. It was a very calm winter's day, so it seemed OK to leave my board alongside the rafts while I stood on the rafts to lower their anchors. Unfortunately, while on the third and final raft, a breath of wind proved just strong enough to leave me stranded. February can be a particularly refreshing month for lake swimming. **Never leave your board unsecured!**

*Crepuscular rays are sometimes seen before sunset, Syvota, Greece.*

# Make the most of the coast

There's something special about the sea. Just a glimpse of it can lift our spirits. A longer look and a listen to the waves can bring a blissful inner calm. Supping offers a fascinating opportunity to appreciate its moods and movements and the intricacies of its edges.

Evenings are particularly inspiring. Individual lines of light, known as crepuscular rays, beam down from the sun at many angles, skimming through the clouds and lighting up the ripples. Later as the sun sets, the clouds become all manner of warm glowing colours, contrasting with the paler blue sky and reflecting on the sea's surface. Having grown up in Derby, 70 miles from the nearest beach, Skegness, I really appreciate living close to the sea now.

Coastlines come in four main types: mud, sand, shingle or rock. Each has their challenges for Suppers and for plants and creatures to live.

Shingle beach, Worbarrow Bay, Dorset.

Sand dune, Instow, Devon.

Muddy saltmarsh, Poole Harbour.

Rocky, Giant's Causeway, Co. Antrim.

# Where there's muck ...

Muddy shores tend to be found where streams and rivers meet the sea and mud is deposited around the shore in estuaries, harbours and lagoons. These provide some of our more sheltered coastal places to paddle, though estuaries can have complex flows.

Being nutrient rich, they support a wealth of invertebrate life including lugworms, ragworms, molluscs and crabs, making them extremely important feeding grounds for wading birds. Redshanks can risk nesting lower on the shore as their chicks float. The whimbrel, with its long down-curved bill for delving the detritus, resembles a small curlew, whereas the bill of the rare black and white avocet (symbol of the RSPB) curves upward for sifting the silt. Bill adaptations don't come stranger than those of spoonbills, another silt sifter. Seeing a flock of these quite large birds in flight makes for a bizarre

Here, in Devon, the rivers Taw and Torridge meet just before reaching the sea. Tide and wind add to the equation.

spectacle. It is a good idea not to paddle too close to waders as some will be desperately trying to conserve and build up energy resources for long migratory flights. Disturbing some seabirds can cause them to abandon their nests, such as the avocet. Otters also frequent these places and are partial to dining on crab.

Such areas are particularly affected by tides, but with good planning and well chosen timing these can be very helpful. We will look more at tides and trip planning later (*see page 119*) as tides can be less co-operative if you get on the wrong side of them. Many a paddler has been left high but not quite dry, with a

Spot the bill competition: Redshank.

Avocet.

Whimbrel.

Spoonbill.

Estuary mud near Appledore, Devon.

flowered sea aster which looks like its American garden relative Michaelmas daisy, both of which are still flowering well on 29 September, Michaelmas Day. Sea-lavender has thick leaves and purple flowers.

The green fleshy finger-leaved glasswort was used in glass-making and is now more known for its culinary use when lightly boiled. It is also known as marsh samphire or simply samphire on menus. It is incredibly tolerant of salty conditions. Try a little raw to see how salty it tastes.

Sea aster among glasswort.

long, leg-strength-sapping wade through sinky, slippery and sometimes smelly mud.

Plants adapted to the challenge of changing water and salinity levels can take advantage of rich nutrients without competition from larger, commoner plants and trees. Salt marshes are popular places for various types of geese, ducks and even deer to forage and graze. If ever places for paddling merited bringing binoculars it is near these habitats.

Some of the specialised species of flora found here are: the purple and yellow

Sea-lavender.

Three Cliffs Bay, The Gower.

Wild cabbage.

Sea rocket.

Sea bindweed.

# Sand dune banks

A good beach can be a great safe sandy-bottomed place to paddle on calm days. It may involve a fair walk through dunes.

Dune systems play an important role in stabilising the sand and rely on a battle hardened front-line of marram grass and the broader-bladed sea lyme grass. The latter has a bluish coating that protects it from salty winds, which comes off if you rub your fingers along it.

Adding more colour to the dunes is sea rocket, which has fleshy leaves and seed heads to cope with salty winds, and flowers that can be white, pink or light purple. Salt tolerant plants, known as halophytes, include several that have been cultivated for vegetables, such as wild cabbage and sea kale as well as sea rocket.

Also look out for the pink and white flowers of sea bindweed and try not to step through the prickly leaved, blue flowered sea holly. Moths are attracted to the bright lemon yellow, night-scented flowers of evening primrose.

Sea holly.

Evening primrose.

Cuttlefish bone.

Cuttlefish alongside paddle.

Mermaid's purse.

Whelk's eggs.

Bladderwrack — nature's bubble-wrap.

# Strandline treasures

The sea itself holds many mysteries. What secrets are stored within? What lies beneath the surface? The strandline leaves an insight into this beautiful marine world with many types of often attractive shells and samples of seaweed, many of which, including the light green sheets of sea lettuce, are edible. Bladderwrack is nature's bubble-wrap with lots of round air pockets to keep it buoyant and to aid photosynthesis.

Shingle beaches are difficult to grow on as the pebbles keep moving, but some of the above plants can get a hold above the strandline. They are also hard to walk on with bare feet, so it's worth wearing neoprene footwear that can be kept on your feet or board or stored in a dry-bag ready for your exit. Once

you reach the water, shingle can shelve more dramatically than sand so it may be trickier getting on and more particularly getting out as the pebbles slide under your feet. Steeper slopes make for bigger waves hitting the shore.

The line of debris left by the retreating tide can be a good place to look for curios, such as cuttlefish 'bones'. Technically these aren't bones, but internal shells used for buoyancy. They would make great paddleboards for crabs, with the high rails of a race board. Place them in the sea (without crabs!) and they will often catch a wave and surf in.

Clumps of whelk's eggs resemble spongy rice cakes and were used as sponges by sailors. Mermaid's purses are the egg cases of rays or dogfish. Over a dozen types can be found around Britain, like this from a thornback ray.

# Rock and pool lifestyles

The beautiful blue viper's bugloss can be found on rocky shores, along with the fleshy golden samphire and pretty pink-flowered thrift. A particularly captivating habitat, providing hours of family fun, are rock pools. They provide living space for some very adaptable creatures as water level, temperature and salinity can change drastically in sun and rain. One of the more colourful inhabitants is the beadlet anemone. These jelly-like rich red blobs retract their tentacles when out of water to reduce surface area and water loss.

Viper's bugloss.

Thrift.

Beadlet anemones in and out of water.

Golden samphire.

*Velvet swimming crab.*

*Edible crab.*

*Shore crab.*

## GET TO KNOW YOUR CRABS

Hiding under rocks around the shoreline are the characterful crabs that crawl sideways to escape sea birds, otters and children with nets. They are one of our most iconic groups of creatures and an important food source for many others. Although rock pool creatures are adaptable many suffer when left in buckets in the hot sun.

● Edible crabs which closely resemble Cornish pasties can grow to become our biggest species, if we don't eat them.

Large specimens can occasionally be seen when looking down from a paddleboard. Restaurants refer to them as brown crabs, though they can be pink or even deep purple.
● The more angular shore crab is our commonest and tends to be greenish as an adult but all manner of colours and patterns when young.
● Another sizeable species is the velvet swimming crab, with broad stripy back legs adapted for swimming. The beady blood-red eyes give a clue to its bold fiery

nature. Crabs are safest to handle from the sides but take care with this one.

● There are several smaller species, including the broad-clawed porcelain crab. It only grows to 5cm, most of which is claw.

● Hermit crabs have soft bodies and hide in empty shells, changing homes as they grow. Their most desirable residence is the shell of the dog whelk.

Crabs shed their skins in order to grow (as shown below). After this they are more vulnerable to attack from predators. Males have to wait until females become softer after shedding their skins before they can mate.

*Gannet with nest material.*

*'Oh, Claude, wait until I've slipped into something more comfortable.'*

*'Sure thing, shore thing.'*

# Close encounters of the bird kind

Out on the water you can make many feathered acquaintances. The dart-like diving terns, such as the common, little and sandwich varieties, all have white bodies and black heads. Northern Europe's largest sea bird, the gannet, also specialises in fast dives. With black wing tips and a yellow head it's a striking bird in more ways than one. Having a wingspan of around 1.8m (6 feet) it is a very powerful flyer and has shock-absorbing adaptations to its head and body to cope with the impact of its dives. In the region of 70% of the world's population nest around the British Isles.

Another distinctive sea bird is the black and white oystercatcher, with a scarlet bill and evocative call. It feeds, not surprisingly, on shellfish.

Gulls begin life looking camouflaged and gradually lose their mottled brown plumage over their first four years.

Oystercatcher.

They include:

- Black-headed gulls with very dark brown heads in summer, but just a small black spot behind the eye in winter. Their legs and bills are reddish.
- Mediterranean gulls are rarer than the above, but are a similar size and, confusingly, do have black heads and much redder legs and bills.
- The larger white and light grey herring gull with pink feet and a splodge of red on its lower bill, like tomato sauce ready to dip your chips into.
- Of similar size with yellow feet and darker grey back is the lesser black-backed gull.

- Noticeably bigger, with pink feet and a very dark grey back, is the ominous looking great black-backed gull.

These last two, like mature herring gulls, also have a noticeable red projection on the lower part of their yellow bills. Its real purpose is food related. The chicks are attracted to it and thereby encouraged to take fish from their parents' bills. It is known as (second bird word alert) the gonys.

There are various rarer birds, including the comical looking puffin, which nest on cliffs and feed out at sea. Binoculars can prove useful if you can keep them dry. It's particularly important not to disturb fragile populations. Not that you'd want to SUP too near nesting areas due to the smell of guano (third bird word alert: if you didn't know, you can guess what it means).

Juvenile black-headed gull with mottled markings.

THE PADDLEBOARD BIBLE

Herring gull with gonys. One way to get the kids to eat.

Mediterranean gull with black head and blood red bill.

# Wildlife etiquette

To keep you safe as well as the wildlife, environmental groups suggest the following guidelines in important nature areas:

- Avoid disturbance to areas used for feeding by overwintering birds as their energy reserves are vital for long migrations.
- Avoid bird breeding areas as disturbance can lead to chicks or eggs being abandoned – keep at least 200m away.
- Don't approach rafting birds or land where large numbers are gathered.
- Embark and disembark at landing points and keep to paths to avoid habitat damage.
- Explore in small groups only.
- Never split a mother from her young.
- With mammals, stay on course so they can predict your movements.
- Move on after 10 minutes watching.
- Let animals decide how close to be.
- Allow animals an escape route – as a group stay to one side.
- Avoid trampling sea bed wildlife.
- I've added this one: don't go nearer than, and definitely don't block the view of, others already watching. Why do some people do that, darn them?!

Wildlife may reward you with moments to relish and memories to cherish.

# Sea mammals

A truly spectacular sight is a pod of bottlenose dolphins. I've had this blessing off Ireland's County Donegal, thanks to my sharp-eyed better half. On the first occasion they were leaping in unison as they moved across the water. On the second, they were performing synchronised acrobatic leaps well above the surface. Porpoise are sometimes seen, but are smaller and generally don't rise out of the water as far.

The first time I joined an organised SUP tour in Poole Harbour, we saw a common dolphin close up. These are a fair bit smaller than the bottlenose, with white undersides and a creamy yellow curved band on their flanks. This poor soul looked disoriented up against a sea wall. Two of the group helped it into deeper water. Generally the advice is not to interfere with cetaceans (whales and dolphins). Their presence can be reported to a relevant wildlife charity such as British Divers Marine Life Rescue (www.bdmlr.org.uk) or the Coast Guard or Local Authority.

*Dolphins sometimes approach paddlers.*

*Paddlers admiring a male bottlenose dolphin.*

BDMLR has guidelines on its website and hotline numbers: 01825 765546 or 07787 433412. They also help seals.

Healthy common dolphins don't tend to come into shallow water. Bottlenose are much more likely to be seen by Suppers. Females, known as 'cows', live in groups or pods, along with calves. Lone males, which are larger and known as 'bulls', come close to shore around May to establish territories while looking for a mate. You might think these sentient cetaceans, blessed with intelligence, grace and beauty, would seek a special connection. The truth seems less romantic. They spread their love around, polygamously, and males can become very pushy when frisky. Occasionally humans have suffered at the flippers of enthusiastic individuals, so take care!

The most likely whale to be seen in our shallower waters is the minke whale. Not a big species by whale standards, but still around 8m long, so you'll know it's a whale! The black and white orca or killer whale grows to around 9.5m. They are occasionally seen around Britain, particularly Scotland, and sometimes prey on the minke. Thankfully they're not known to attack humans in the wild.

As a Supper you are probably more likely to see seals, with our two main species being the grey seal with a more

*Lengthy leviathans — orcas can reach almost 10m.*

Common seal and pup.

pointed 'Roman nose' and the smaller, though still sizeable, common or harbour seal with a rounded face and a nose more reminiscent of a labrador. They can be curious, even playful, but stay at least 70m away unless they approach you on their own terms, especially if there is a group of you. Their bite is more powerful than any dog's, so not great for your board for one thing. If you kneel or sit on your board and only paddle gently, they will be less alarmed by your presence and if you're fortunate they may come to see you on their terms. They have tried mounting paddleboards, which makes balancing tricky!

Seals are curious. According to TV naturalist Simon King, they will sometimes come closer to investigate if you sing. This may work with seals and certain cetaceans, but usually has the opposite effect on other wildlife and possibly fellow Suppers! I'm not sure which songs and singers tend to gain seal approval.

One beautiful winter's day, I was paddling between the RSPB's Arne Reserve and a couple of islands in Poole Harbour. Twice a seal's head popped up very close to me, then on the third occasion, while I was in very shallow water this beautiful beast came out of the water alongside me as if gradually trying to befriend me. They do seem to recognise individual people, if they have the chance to become acquainted.

This common seal leapt on the SUP enthusiastically and adeptly.

# Other points of interest

As well as wildlife, Supping provides opportunities to see historic features from unusual angles, from major castles to small details on bridges. Water has played such an important part in our past.

Paddling is also a great way to see geological features, such as arches, sea stacks, caves and contorted bedding planes. The two photos below show features on the Jurassic Coast, World Heritage Site, Dorset. Some of these can be a tricky test of manoeuvring skills with the potential to scratch boards and paddles. That said, it would be a great way to inspire interest on geography field trips and to study processes like longshore drift and the development of rivers.

Paddlers at Pembroke Castle.

Durdle Door, natural arch on Dorset's Jurassic Coast.

Pinnacle like an ice cream by Old Harry Rocks, further east on Dorset's Jurassic Coast.

# Wildlife around the world

Red-throated diver or loon.

We are indebted to the USA for starting the National Park movement in the late 19th century, with Yellowstone the first to be designated. A tempting destination for any Supping naturalist is the Florida Keys, where the abundant marine life includes stingrays and manatees. Along with some jaw-dropping landscapes, North America has much notable wildlife. Western Canada is particularly worthy of exploration. As well as beavers, we saw moose, elk, black bears and osprey while paddling inland. Off the coast bald eagles, seals and even whales are worth looking out for. Paddling on lakes you will often see birds known there as 'loons', such as the red-throated loon. Birds are often less restricted to land masses than other wildlife and in Britain we call loons 'divers'.

Some South and Central American countries, such as Brazil, have incredible biodiversity, albeit under threat. Costa Rica is a leading light in protecting wild areas and its tourism industry and economy benefits accordingly. Sloths and various monkeys can be seen in Mario Antonio National Park on the Pacific coast and there's a great beach for SUP surfing just to the north. There are even organised SUP trips among the Galapagos, the islands west of Ecuador that inspired Darwin's great work *On the Origin of Species*.

Africa also has some amazing wildlife, including hippos and crocodiles and other big beasts that visit the waterways and

Black bear and cubs, Vancouver Island, Western Canada.

Costa Rican Caiman.

Plumed basilisk lizard, Costa Rica.

Duck-billed platypus.
Paddle with a living riddle.

Australian pelican.

watering holes. The Victoria Falls might not be the only hazardous highlight of a trip down the Zambezi! At least Europe's wildlife is not particularly threatening to paddlesport enthusiasts.

Known particularly for its threatened populations of ground nesting birds, such as the kiwi, New Zealand also has the sacred kingfisher, which nests in riverbanks and is similar in shape but a little less colourful than the European species.

Sacred kingfishers are also found in other countries south east of the Wallace Line (which distinguishes between countries with wildlife of Australian origin and those with Asian lineage), including Australia, which also has the more vividly coloured azure kingfisher. The bird sounds here are particularly evocative and exotic with the Eastern whip bird's whooping whistle and the onomatopoeic laugh-like call of the kookaburra, which is also in the kingfisher family. Australian swans are black with red bills. A particularly peculiar bird is the pelican, though they aren't just found in Australia, with eight species occurring around the world including the large handsome white and black Australian pelican.

When it comes to charismatic, enigmatic wildlife, Australia stands tall with its marsupials and the weird, wonderful water-based duck-billed platypus, which grow much bigger in Tasmania than on the mainland. On quiet eastern waterways, at dawn or dusk or on dull days, listen for the splash as they enter the water and look for them surfacing or the bow wave as they swim.

Australia has its fair share of dangerous species such as mighty saltwater crocodiles and sharks. It also has some great place names. While working on a wildlife research project in Croajingolong National Park, in Victoria, I went for a long barefoot beach walk to the first location Captain Cook discovered on mainland Australia. After walking 12km and with the return trip ahead of (and behind) me, I worryingly almost trod on a small scorpion on the sand. Thankfully for me there isn't a sting in this tale, though their several species of scorpions don't tend to be life threatening.

Be wary but not deterred, it is a wonderful country to explore. The water is typically the temperature of bath water including that in the longest river, the Murray, as it forms a wide warm paddle-worthy boundary between New South Wales and the north west of Victoria. Australia is also famous for stunning surf beaches.

Sharks are beautiful, fascinating creatures that are being killed for their fins for soup at an alarming and unsustainable rate – however, you don't want to be part of a statistic in the other direction. Fortunately many species prefer

plankton or crustaceans to paddleboarders. Tips for reducing the risk of becoming a shark's supper (sorry, poor taste!):

- Don't paddle alone, especially early mornings and late evenings (popular feeding time).
- Avoid river mouths.
- If you see shoals of fish, which may attract sharks, leave the water.
- If you see a shark, leave the water quickly.
- Try to remain calm and remember your technique.
- If in a group, stay together.
- Above all try to paddle with people a little slower than you!

Sharks rarely attack when the water is cooler than 20° Celsius. Suddenly Britain and Ireland become appealing SUP destinations!

Risks accepted, there is a whole world of wildlife, with numerous natural niches and riches in and around the planet's water bodies, and Supping is a superb way to witness it.

*Well, his paddle was the wrong way around!*

# 6 STAND UP FOR 'SUPWAYS'

There might not be much intertidal range to land on.

# Access

Access to water can be a murky grey area with several shades. Fortunately kayakers and canoeists, and bodies such as British Canoeing (BC) that represent them, have been trying to establish access and smooth the waters. In 2019 the BC website launched its 'Go Paddling' page with updated information detailing places to paddle and trails to follow.

If a body of water has been paddled for years then it's probably OK to take your paddleboard on it, though some lakes may have an arrangement with a particular group. Some areas are zoned for different recreational uses. Busy beaches, for instance, may have designated safe swimming zones where the RNLI provide cover. Other watersports are not permitted in these but

can go around the outside of them. Never go out on a beach with a red flag flying. A good relationship with the RNLI is particularly important as they will play a part in decisions and we may rely on them in times of need.

We also need to take great care in designated areas for other watersports as well as shipping lanes. Some areas are particularly important for wildlife and various guidelines have been produced for these, including those under the 'Wildlife etiquette' heading (*see page 101*).

You may be able to take a break without landing, like this Easyriders group.

SUP past Kilchurn Castle on the 'Go Paddling' Loch Awe Challenge.

*Take care near cliffs.*

in a way that respects people's privacy.

Land isn't always accessible and sometimes it would be very unwise to land, for instance, near an eroding cliff or slope. Areas used by the military as a base or for training may also be 'no go'. Some may only be out of bounds when training is taking place, but others may be generally unsafe. In such areas you may see a beach inaccessible from the land, which seems a very tempting place to stop, but it may have unexploded ordnance. It's well worth looking out for signage, speaking to locals and finding out what restrictions apply and when.

## Coast

Land between low and high tide is often owned by the Crown Estate, though owners of adjoining land above high tide don't always see it as being accessible to the public. Private landowners sometimes put signs up to this effect. Much coastal land above the foreshore is owned by the relevant local authority and tends to be OK to access. If you're thoughtful and polite it helps and you can raft up just off shore as an option. Finding out about land ownership is often difficult. Sometimes you just have to judge how likely landing would be to cause offence and behave

## Inland

Lakes will tend to be owned by someone or an organisation, or be publicly owned and managed by the local council, though this doesn't necessarily mean paddling is allowed. If it is owned by a statutory body, such as a water company or local authority, it will generally be reasonably easy to find out if access is permitted. It may be possible to gain access on some sort of basis, maybe for a club or an event. Some lakes or zones within lakes are accessible to Suppers, though launching and landing may be restricted to certain places. For some lakes, like one in Cotswold Water Park, there is a charge to SUP even if using your own board.

Some areas will have seasonal access. For instance, Loch Levan north of Edinburgh is a National Nature Reserve partly because of its over-wintering birds, but access is allowed from April to September. On the whole, access is much better north of the border, thanks to the Land Reform (Scotland) Act 2003. Here, responsible, considerate access to paddle is the norm both on inland waters and the coast.

Navigable lengths of canals are generally accessible. A British Canoeing 'waterways licence' provides access to those owned by the Canal and River Trust, The Environment Agency and the Broads Authority (for the Norfolk Broads, though alternatively you can obtain a Broads Authority Licence). You'll need to find somewhere to launch and land safely. You may also need to carry your equipment around locks and in some areas cope with busy traffic. People on canal boats and lock keepers are generally a friendly bunch.

Tidal and navigable stretches of rivers also tend to be OK for paddleboarders, though look out for signs. British Canoeing, with Rivers Publishing, have produced a

The Grand Union Canal, London.

helpful map showing stretches where it's OK to paddle on rivers and canals, but there are other areas it may be OK too and they are campaigning for greater access. The UK Rivers Guidebook website (www.ukriversguidebook.co.uk) gives updates on the condition of some rivers, whether there are any issues and whether local people are welcoming to paddlers.

Access to riverbanks can be subject to landowner permission or local bylaws but is not a general right. Where rivers aren't navigable by boats, they can provide some of our most idyllic peaceful paddling with a chance to explore stretches that don't have footpath or bridleway access or where walkers only see glimpses of the water. Paddling these 'SUPways' can be a great way to find wild swimming opportunities. It's a shame that access to these areas is often limited or unclear.

Some people are lucky enough to have gardens backing onto rivers: a Supper's dream. Try not to disturb them or invade

Place to SUP or dip.

their privacy, especially as paddleboards afford a higher view than kayaks. Often riverside inhabitants enjoy watching the world go by along with occasional paddlers. Sometimes they wave, though try not to fall in as you reciprocate. Maybe a few hope you will! If you have a friendly demeanour people will naturally tend to at least be civil, even if they have objections.

If people canoe or kayak then Supping should be OK, but keep in mind that we have fixed fins and check maps for weirs, particularly if the flow is fast. It may be possible to walk around them, but not guaranteed. Some signs may say 'No kayaks, no swimming'. They may have been installed by landowners or fishing clubs. If they don't mention SUPs, it's probably because we're relatively new and it's safe to assume we wouldn't receive a warm welcome either.

A special licence is required to paddle on some areas such as the Thames in London, though organisers of events such as races will make arrangements for this if you're not a member of British Canoeing or it isn't covered.

According to British Canoeing, 'Of the 42,700 miles of inland waterways in England, only 1,400 miles can be paddled uncontested – that is a mere 4% of what is available. Paddlers are subject to challenge or dispute over their right to be on the water. The 4% of waterways is largely made up of canals and "managed navigations" (such as the Wye and the Severn).' In November 2018, British Canoeing launched a campaign called 'Clear Access Clear Water', with videos featuring multiple Paralympic and World Champion Emma Wiggs MBE, paddleboarder and environmental campaigner Cal Major and TV presenter and naturalist Steve Backshall on their website at: www.britishcanoeing.org.uk/ go-canoeing/access-and-environment/ access-charter-campaign

This promotes fair, shared and sustainable open access to water for all, so everyone can appreciate and care about our waterways and we all benefit. When I contacted Ben Seal, BC's Places to Paddle Manager, which sounds like a great job title, he informed me:

*Where can we paddle?*

*River access is something to celebrate.*

PRIVATE PROPERTY
No Hydrofoils
No Jet Skis
No Spear Fishing
No Drone Flying
Thank you

*Hopefully SUP will keep a good level of access.*

'The campaign is going well. We are steadily building our support cross party; meeting MPs and Ministers and working on solutions with DEFRA. More importantly we are building support within the paddling community – and beyond with swimmers and other folks who care for our waterways. Protection of the environment is a key driver for greater access, so we are working hard to promote this angle, getting paddlers to undertake river cleans all over the country. The SUP community seem particularly engaged, so this is a big area where we can win support for Clear Access, Clear Waters.'

Clarity on the laws affecting river access would be really helpful. It can seem like a can of worms (or maggots!). The better our reputation as Suppers, the more chance we stand of positive decisions being made that provide us with good levels of access. As the relatively new kid in school, this is particularly important, but at least we have the opportunity to build good relationships. Hopefully goodwill we create will flow back our way from Westminster.

# Access around the world

Access rights, not surprisingly, vary from country to country. There are often exceptions to general rules due to local or national laws.

Norway, Sweden and Finland have their versions of a right to roam similar to Scotland's under the concept of 'Everyman's Rights'. France has a generally accepted right of navigation, subject to local bylaws relating to the area. The water in their many kilometres of navigable rivers is publicly owned but permission to access it or land will depend on adjoining land ownership. In Belgium there is widespread permission to paddle on rivers, subject to some accommodations for the fishing season, flow rates and environmental issues. There is also a general right of navigation in Hungary and Bulgaria.

The USA, Australia and New Zealand have a public right of navigation and good levels of access. In Canada this has evolved as an unwritten rule to which restrictions can be applied, for instance by Act of Parliament. The National

Organization for Rivers campaigns for river access in the US.

There is no substitute for local knowledge as to how legislation is interpreted and applied. In parts of some countries crocodiles may enjoy the final word on the matter.

# Voluntary work

One way to enhance our standing is to organise or take part in voluntary work. This could involve litter-picking on the shore, from the bank or in the water. Take care as most paddleboards aren't as robust as some kayaks and canoes. Damaging your best board in an effort to pick up a piece of litter someone else may have thoughtlessly dropped is annoying. Moving in and out of vegetation, particularly on flowing water, is also a challenge.

Suppers have set up campaigns including Planet Patrol (https://planetpatrol.co) initiated by Lizzie Carr. They may be able to help you organise

Shot through the heart... Single-Use-Plastics give a good acronym a bad name! Lizzie Carr on a plastic raft.

a litter pick in your area. You can also download their free litter tracking app, Planet Patrol, and be a citizen scientist on your SUP adventures, gathering vital data to help solve plastic pollution and littering. There's also Paddle Against Plastic (www.paddleagainstplastic.com) co-ordinated by Cal Major who featured on BBC2's *Springwatch* series. Notable SUP adventures have fuelled the motivation of them both, as well as demanding a lot of their own clean, green energy.

Organising a litter pick is a good opportunity to invite and meet different SUP and canoe clubs in your area. Other groups could help with picking the banks. A local fishing club may be interested and this could facilitate access, on the day at least, to different stretches of river. It may lead to building bridges with anglers! Ask the local authority if they can collect your pickings or provide bags, gloves or litter-picking tools. Many paddlers, being good citizens, pick up a few items of rubbish whenever they paddle or walk.

Particularly interesting and satisfying work is river restoration. This involves restoring the meanders and habitats within straightened sections of rivers by staking logs to the river bed or using brushwood to produce bends and cover. The effects on the flow can be seen instantly, giving a great insight into how rivers move, which is useful to paddleboarders. County Wildlife Trusts and other charities with an interest in rivers sometimes organise these tasks.

Another task is Himalayan balsam pulling. This introduced plant is taking over the banks of many rivers and lakes. It has pretty pink flowers, which bees like to enter and the exploding seed heads can provide a fun shock when knocked, so people didn't realise what a problem it would become. Its seed-spreading trick has enabled it to cover long lengths of some of our waterways, leading to the

Collect some litter on your SUP, all day long, you'll have good luck!

*Giving the river more wildlife interest.*

September and is a good excuse to relive your childhood. Training is often provided by a county-wide co-ordinator. If the figures vary dramatically it shows up changes to the river's health. I sample within a farm that operates as a public attraction. Families visiting think I'm an activity laid on by the company that runs the farm and they all want to join in.

# Biosecurity and invasive species

When plant and animal species are introduced from other countries, some can't cope with their new conditions, some can and remain a part of a balanced ecosystem, but some become problem species. These not only cope, but lacking the controls and predators that keep them in check in their natural niches, they

loss of our native plants. These would collectively provide nectar for a wider variety of insects over a much longer flowering season as well as displaying a whole range of colours and forms.

The other problem is that after balsam has set seed it dies back for the winter, leaving exposed banks, which suffer from erosion in winter storms. The sediment in the rivers causes many problems, particularly for salmon and trout, which require clean gravel to breed and clear water for the young to develop. By pulling up the menace before it sets seed we can give other plants a chance. Many hands can make a big impact.

The Riverfly Partnership (www.riverflies.org) involves volunteers surveying a convenient river location by counting how many of several invertebrate species are present. This means rummaging through the water with a net once a month from April to

*Invasive Himalayan balsam.*

spread rapidly causing havoc with the balance of nature in their new environment.

Plants taking over our still and slow-flowing water bodies include floating water fern from South America, parrot's feather – also from South America – and Australian swamp stonewort. A small frond or fragment of any of these transported, perhaps on the grippy bit of a board, to another water body can become a huge problem.

By checking your equipment after a paddle, cleaning/rinsing it and allowing it to dry, you're not only looking after your kit, but also the environment. This is promoted as the 'Check, Clean, Dry' procedure.

A particularly saddening problem is the plight of our native white-clawed crayfish. As a child I often found, and marveled at, these freshwater lobsters. Now they have been wiped out of most of Britain's streams and rivers by a plague spread by the American signal crayfish.

One of the few rivers in Dorset where they were hanging on, was the River Allen. Although signal crayfish have not been found there, the plague was discovered a few years ago and within a very short time our white-clawed were all gone.

If you regularly move from one river to another with equipment and one of the rivers still supports native crayfish, cleaning gear with a chemical called Virkon is recommended. This disinfectant comes in tablets that dissolve in warm water that can then be sprayed and/or scrubbed on equipment. If you're lucky enough to live near fresh and salty water, alternating between them can help too.

Marine habitats are not free from invasives. On some British beaches 90% of the shells are those of the American slipper limpet. These party animals like to get together and living clusters can be completely washed up after wild stormy nights (many of us know the feeling!). There's also a brown seaweed known as Japanese wireweed clogging some coasts that makes paddling arduous and can grow 10cm in a day up to a length of 10m. *The Day of the Triffids* looms.

*American slipper limpets including clusters.*

# 7 THE ELEMENTS

*The Moon, being much closer, exerts around twice the pull of the Sun on our oceans.*

# Tides

When the Moon and Sun are aligned in the same direction from the Earth (new moon) or opposite directions (full moon), the gravitational pulls combine to produce bigger tides, known as 'spring tides'. When the Sun and Moon are at 90 degrees to each other in relation to the Earth, we see 'half moons' and smaller 'neap tides'.

Tides vary on a daily, monthly and annual basis:

● **Daily** – the Earth spins on its axis (poles) every 24 hours. This would produce two high tides and two lows. However, tidal flows are affected by land masses such as islands, large rivers and reefs.

● **Monthly** – this is caused by the Moon orbiting the Earth and, as already described, produces spring and neap tides. One orbit takes around 29 and a half days.

● **Annual variations** occur due to the Moon's elliptical orbiting pattern. The biggest tides occur around the spring and autumn equinoxes, in late March and late September, when the Moon is closer. There are also supertides every 18.6 years due to the Moon's position in relation to the Earth.

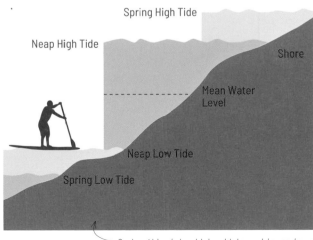

Spring High Tide
Neap High Tide
Shore
Mean Water Level
Neap Low Tide
Spring Low Tide

*Spring tides bring higher highs and lower lows.*

*Wind turbines, Brazil.*

*Tide and time. High tide will be 50 minutes later tomorrow.*

Tides don't happen at the same time from one day to the next. This is because the Moon is pulling the tidal bulge from a slightly different position each day. If there was a high tide at 1pm today, tomorrow it will be at around 1.50pm.

Unlike the weather, tides are predictable and tidal predictions are available as tables and charts in booklets and on the internet. The booklets are available each year for a few pounds. The charts show the tides in graphic form. If you live in an area where land masses,

such as islands, mean the tides aren't straight-forward sine waves, the charts are very useful. They are slightly more expensive, but many people find graphs easier to understand than tables. *Reeds Nautical Almanac*, produced annually, provides the definitive guide to tidal information.

Online tide predictions are available on the Easytide website: www.ukho.gov. uk/easytide. These give data and graphic predictions which are free for the current week ahead. Other sites also show the

SPRING TIDES

Full Moon                    Or New Moon

High Tide    Low Tide    High Tide

Low Tide

Sun

*Tidal bulge diagram.*

NEAP TIDES

1st Quarter Half Moon

High Tide

Low Tide    Low Tide

High Tide

Sun

3rd Quarter Half Moon

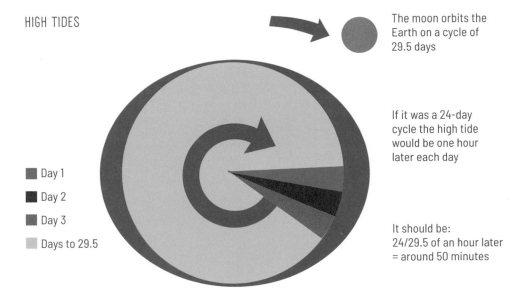

The moon orbits the Earth on a cycle of 29.5 days

If it was a 24-day cycle the high tide would be one hour later each day

It should be:
24/29.5 of an hour later
= around 50 minutes

- ■ Day 1
- ■ Day 2
- ■ Day 3
- ■ Days to 29.5

expected tide graphically and in figures, including Magic Seaweed, which features live webcams so you can see the lie of the water: www.magicseaweed.com

Tides can have major horizontal effects where the water level changes significantly. This can leave you with a long walk back across exposed shore if returning at low tide. On a very gently sloping coast this can happen even with small drops in water level. It can also lead to problems if embarking from a sea wall.

The difference between the height of consecutive low and high tides is known as the 'tidal range'. For example (where chart datum is the lowest astronomical tide possible):

|  |  | Height above Chart Datum (m) |
|---|---|---|
| High tide | Spring | 6 |
|  | Neap | 5 |
| Low tide | Neap | 2 |
|  | Spring | 1 |

*Poole Harbour has a small tidal range; it can still mean a long walk at low tide.*

Tidal range:

**Spring** = 6-1 = 5m
**Neap**   = 5-2 = 3m

Local topography can have a major effect on tide patterns and ranges. The biggest tidal ranges occur where the tide is funneled by the landform. The Bay of Fundy in Nova Scotia produces a range of a whopping 15m.

Tides also have significant vertical effects, for example where water travels up a river. The downstream flow of the river will gradually become the dominant factor or the tidal flow may be stopped by a weir. The tides can help both ways with a well-timed estuary paddle.

Closer to home, one of the most substantial ranges in the world occurs where the tidal waters are squeezed up the Bristol Channel and into the River Severn Estuary. On spring tides this produces a range of up to 13m and a current known as the Severn Bore

travelling up the river, overcoming two weirs near Gloucester and sometimes one at Tewkesbury. There can be a delay of over an hour after high tide on the sea before stretches up a river reach their highest water level.

The bore waves are a well-known phenomenon to surfers and were first surfed in 1955 by World War Two veteran Lieutenant-Colonel Jack Churchill on a board he designed himself. A few 5 foot (1.5m) waves were never going to faze 'Mad Jack', who survived many heroic exploits during the war, for which he received the Military Cross.

Tide tables are only predictions and wind can have a major effect. For example, the Severn Bore is bigger with a south-westerly wind.

The rate of tidal flow changes throughout the tide cycle. This is known as the 'Rule of Twelfths'. Between a high and low tide, of the outflowing water: 1/12th flows out in the first hour,

*The River Wye at Chepstow.*

2/12ths in the 2nd, 3/12ths in the 3rd, 3/12ths in the 4th, 2/12ths in the 5th and 1/12th in the 6th and the reverse of this as it flows back in (*see chart on next page*). So around high and low tides the flow is slow, but between them it races by comparison.

In Poole Harbour there is a large bay, called Lytchett Bay, separated from the main body of water as it flows under a railway bridge, which acts as a pinch point. At high tide you can play games under the bridge, but 3 hours before this it can be a real struggle to come out. In the tidal race, 3 hours after high tide, a kneeling paddler can be flushed out of the

*Surfers on the Severn Bore.*

*The Forth Bridge. Where estuaries are large with significant tidal ranges, paddlers need calm conditions, experience and very careful planning.*

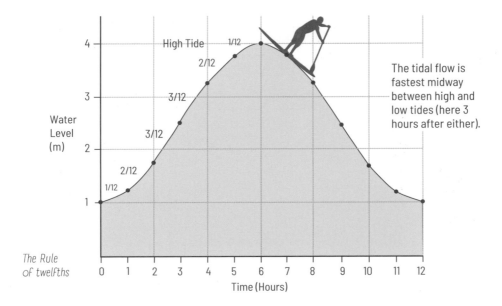

Water Level (m)

High Tide

1/12
2/12
3/12
3/12
2/12
1/12

The tidal flow is fastest midway between high and low tides (here 3 hours after either).

*The Rule of twelfths*

Time (Hours)

bay and easily knocked off balance, but at low tide you can become stranded in the bay wading through thick mud. So it is well worth consulting the tide predictions.

Where tides rush through inlet and estuary entrances they are sometimes known as rip tides. Not to be confused with rip currents (*see page 128*), which are a potentially hazardous phenomenon of beaches, particularly surf beaches or where streams enter a bay.

Parts of the south coast of Britain experience tides affected by the shape of shorelines, including the shelter of the Isle of Wight and the effects of the north

## TOP TIP

Beware pinch points, especially from large bays.

*Lytchett Bay pinch point.*

French coast on the English Channel. This creates a double high tide followed by a particularly rapid outflow on parts of the English south coast, rather than a smooth sine wave of tides. Using the Easytide website shows how this effect manifests itself on the East Dorset coast around Poole, compared to other locations.

There are charts to show how tides behave, for instance around islands such as the Isle of Wight. These are well worth purchasing if you paddle there. As the tides rise along the Channel they flow eastwards until they meet incoming tides flowing south down the east coast. These tidal flows can have a significant effect on paddles along these coasts.

As well as wind, air pressure affects tides. Standard pressure at sea level is 1013 hectopascals (hPa). These used to be called millibars. The higher the air pressure, the lower the sea will be by 1cm for each hPa. The lowest pressure recorded around the British Isles was 925hPa so the sea would have been 88cm higher. This is exceptional but a rise of 30cm would not be unusual. Low pressure generally means less settled weather so this effect adds to the problems of storms and the likelihood of flooding.

Water temperature can also have an effect on tide height. When the water is very warm it can be higher by up to around 15cm.

Chart datum does not take account of wind, temperature or pressure. It is the lowest expected tide based on the position of the Moon, Sun and other astronomical bodies, under average meteorological conditions.

Swell with some chop at Bundoran, Co. Sligo on Ireland's west coast.

# Waves and currents

As the wind blows on the sea, it forces up folds and wrinkles. There are two main types of waves: chop and swell.

**Chop** is caused by the winds in the area where it arises and the waves seem to come from all directions, so it's unpredictable. If you squat more and the chop isn't too high, with good balance you'll be able to cope. It can also make it quite hard to dig your paddle in the right amount and occasionally a wave can catch your paddle unexpectedly, adding to the fun/challenge.

**Swell** consists of waves that continue after the wind that caused them or beyond the area where they were formed. The west side of Britain tends to experience more. Swell depends on:

- Wind speed.
- The duration it blows.
- The distance over which it blows, known as 'fetch'.

Chop at Durdle Door, Dorset.

TOP TIP

Remember not to paddle parallel to the waves.

These three factors determine how big the folds become. Gusts will vary the waves, but over time the small ones will combine to produce larger ones in patterns. These will include sets of bigger waves. The number of these will vary.

Although swell is fairly uniform like a sine wave, if the waves are of any size they can be quite unnerving for less experienced Suppers.

Two or more independently produced swells may combine. When they are in sync with each other it may produce sets of even larger waves. When they are out of phase, comparative lulls occur. Patterns can occur in sets, such as a set of relatively small waves, then one with larger waves followed by a third set with the biggest waves before the cycle repeats. Experienced surfers will read the patterns to select the waves of the height they want. It's good to observe the waves to begin with, as well as asking local surfers and Suppers.

When localised winds are also present this adds to the challenge. One moment you're down, with some shelter, the next

Swell serves surfers well!

*Waves can double up near walls. Take care, especially near marina entrances.*

you're up and exposed to the full force. Winds affect established waves as follows:

● **An onshore wind** will blow the tops off waves, breaking them down.
● **Offshore winds** make waves steeper, rearing up then crashing down as they break.

Where swell and chop combine it is as if the two are superimposed on each other. The height of the swell and the unpredictability of the chop, sometimes adding to the height, makes balancing very challenging.

Windy conditions require more leg work. You'll use them more to balance as well as squatting more. It may help to have your paddle around 5cm shorter in waves than when you're Supping in calm conditions. The length and shape of your board will also be a factor. A board with a curved profile can help. With

less curved boards a longer one may fare better depending on the wavelength.

Wind will have less tendency to form waves where it blows in the same direction as the tidal flow. To summarise their combined effects:

● **Wind with tide** = stronger current in one direction.
● **Wind against tide** = water surface more affected by waves.

Even on a canal or river, when the wind blows the opposite way to the current it will push up ripples. Your board will make a rhythmic sound as you paddle over them with a slightly juddering motion.

As waves approach the coast they are affected by the shape of the sea floor. They slow down, the wavelength shortens and the height increases.

On a good surf beach of average slope the waves will tend to break in a depth of water around 1.3 times

### TOP TIP

Landform will affect waves. Remember not to stay close to sea walls or rocks where reflected waves can double in height, though the sheltered side will give you protection.

*'Picking up good vibrations' to give a Beach Boys citation. Wind against flow on the Thames.*

will cause bow waves, proportional to their size and speed. The shape of the sea bed and the tides and currents can affect waves, but usually waves on the surface of the ocean are produced by wind.

# Rip currents

Surf beaches develop a sand bar parallel to the shore and a little way out from it, with deeper water inshore and offshore of it. Water coming up the beach will spread sideways until it starts to flow back into the water and then form a rip current through the water. These may be stronger if they combine with freshwater draining through a channel on the beach. Here there can be permanent locations for rips, which may also occur near groynes or rocks where the spreading water builds up. Elsewhere rips may change position. As the tide goes out on a sandy beach you may be able to see how the water flows back in from the patterns it leaves on the sand, particularly near rocks.

the height of the waves, so a 50cm wave will tend to break in 65cm of water. If the beach slopes very gently, they will tend to break earlier and crumble. If the slope is steep or there's a rocky shelf or reef they will pitch in shallower water or over rocks, so as soon as you catch the wave your fins catch the bottom.

Where landforms such as headlands or underwater rocks affect the flow of water, the added effects of tides and wind can produce some very interesting wave effects.

Earthquakes may on occasions cause some exceptional waves. Ships and boats

Rip currents will force a gap through the sand bar and can flow out to sea very rapidly. You would have to be

*Wave breaking on rocks.*

*Shingle beaches often shelve steeply at the shore so waves break too near the shore to surf.*

Water flowing on a beach.

Water running back along rocks.

Michael Phelps to make any slight progress trying to swim against them. Unfortunately this is the natural urge: to try swimming back to shore. Swimmers get into difficulty and sometimes drown in rip currents.

The trick is to swim parallel to the shore and out of the rip sideways. Strong swimmers can swim out at 45° toward the shore. Experienced paddlesport enthusiasts use rips as a way of getting beyond the waves without having to battle through them. This requires competence and caution as rips can sweep you out over a hundred metres. Once through the waves you can break out sideways. The other option is to wait for a lull between sets of waves. The top of a rip on the beach is known as the feeder which then sweeps into a narrower neck before widening out and losing speed.

**TOP TIP**

When coming back in, avoid places where the water looks different with eerily flat channels and deeper, darker or discoloured water as this can indicate a rip current.

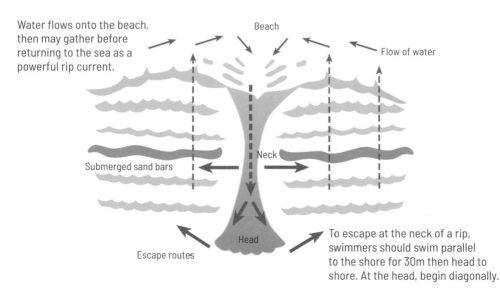

Water flows onto the beach, then may gather before returning to the sea as a powerful rip current.

Beach

Flow of water

Submerged sand bars

Neck

Escape routes

Head

To escape at the neck of a rip, swimmers should swim parallel to the shore for 30m then head to shore. At the head, begin diagonally.

# Weather

The weather can have a major effect on paddling. It will affect:

- Whether you paddle.
- Your choice of location.
- Your route/activity.
- What you wear/pack.
- Your safety and enjoyment.

High pressure is usually good for paddling with slow moving systems, no dramatic changes and settled weather – my, oh my, what wonderful days! Cloud cover will generally be light or absent with little precipitation. Clear skies at night may lead to marked temperature drops with the possibility of fog, particularly in late autumn and winter. When areas of high pressure meet, dry periods may be broken by thunderstorms.

Low pressure systems are unstable, being a contrasting mixture of warm and cold air masses. Typically weather maps will show 'lows' with close concentric isobars bringing stormy winds. These systems are appropriately referred to as depressions and are less happy times for Suppers.

## Fronts

Children pulling funny faces are sometimes told 'if the wind changes you'll be stuck like that'. I don't think it was just me! The cause of a change may well be a 'front' arriving, where different air masses meet. These are shown as lines cutting through the isobars on a weather map.

Where cold air is undercutting warm air it is termed a cold front and clouds will slope steeply. A warm front, where advancing warm air slides above cold, will have gently sloping clouds.

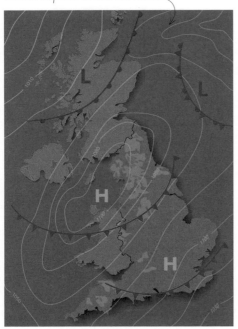

Weather map with isobars and fronts.

If there is a sudden alteration in the wind direction and/or strength, sometimes accompanied by an abrupt drop in temperature and clouds arranged at an angle of 45° or higher, it may be time for a quick rethink of your plans. Not only might the route you had planned become unwise, but cold fronts are usually accompanied by heavy rain and often thunder. Returning to shore, albeit with a sad or permanently funny face, may prove the sensible option.

If you become a regular Supper, you'll find yourself becoming more in tune with what the weather is doing generally and more aware of cloud patterns and their associated climate.

## KIMMERIDGE BAY

This photo, with glassy sea, was the calm before the storm. I was itching for a paddle after working inside on a fine, sunny afternoon. While I pumped up my board the clouds were coming in rapidly but the sea surface was still like glass. I began from Kimmeridge Bay, where Dorset Wildlife Trust has its Wild Seas Centre. Almost as soon as I paddled out of the bay, the wind whipped up, the water went from flat to choppy and the temperature fell. I headed in after only 10 minutes' Supping and landed just in time for a torrential shower to rinse my kit.

Calm at Kimmeridge Bay.

# Wind

Wind is something of a recurring theme in this book, but it has a significant effect on Suppers. There are four main factors that influence the strength and direction of the wind:

● **Differences in barometric pressure.** Air in high pressure areas (highs) is drawn toward areas of low pressure (lows) creating wind flows.

● **The rotation of the Earth.** In the northern hemisphere winds spin clockwise around highs and anticlockwise around lows. The opposite happens below the equator. Air flowing toward the poles creates westerly winds. Air flowing from the poles produces cold northeasterly winds in the northern hemisphere and southeasterlies in the southern. The Earth's rotation will tend to bend winds more to the east (westerlies). This is known as the 'Coriolis effect'.

● **Friction from the Earth's surface** will slow the wind very little over the oceans, but on land it will have a greater effect and the topography may deflect it.

● **Local winds, including sea breezes.** Every paddler should be aware of how these work, so they are worthy of explanation below.

SEA BREEZE BLOWS ONSHORE BY DAY On sunny days, as warm air rises off the land, it is replaced by air drawn off the sea, creating an onshore breeze.

SEA BREEZE BLOWS OFFSHORE BY NIGHT At night cool air over land sinks and is drawn over the sea where the air is now relatively warmer, so less dense.

## LOCAL WINDS

On glorious days for a coastal SUP, the Sun beats down and the sea heats up. As the water moves and mixes it keeps absorbing more warmth. Nearby land warms up at the surface but far less of the Sun's heat is taken in, even though sand can become uncomfortably hot to walk on.

Consequently, the air over the land warms up much more as less heat is absorbed. Hot air rises as with hot air balloons. The air rising above the land creates a vacuum which sucks in the air off the sea. This creates an onshore breeze. This builds up during the heat of the day, peaking around

**SEA BREEZE FROM BOTH SIDES OF A HEADLAND COMBINE**
Onshore winds on different sides of a headland will converge.

**SEA BREEZE AND GENERAL WIND COMBINE**
These local and general winds will combine to produce a south westerly.

Southerly onshore local wind

General wind running westerly along coast

3pm. This could help you to return from a well-timed paddle on a hot day.

Where there is a promontory of land jutting into the sea, breezes from both sides will combine to blow inland. For example in Cornwall sea breezes from north and south of the peninsula converge over the higher ground of Bodmin Moor. Moisture in them condenses as it rises, leading to heavy convectional rainfall. Named after the county's highest hill, this phenomenon is known as the 'Brown Willy effect'.

When there is a general wind blowing along the coast, it will combine with the onshore breeze. For example, a general wind blowing from the south will join forces with an onshore breeze from the west to produce a southwesterly. If the general wind and onshore breeze come from the same direction it will produce a stronger wind that way.

# WATERSPOUTS

One unusual feature, known as a waterspout, can occur where a strong downdraught spirals down in a vortex from the base of a cumulonimbus cloud. They look a bit like a mini-tornado and a swirl of spray is thrown up around the point where it hits the water. Although more common in the tropics, they do occur in Europe including Britain. They can damage small boats so if you see a waterspout making a steady path across the water below a funnel of cloud, try to dodge it!

*Croatian waterspout.*

It is sometimes possible to find sheltered areas in the lee of a cliff, buildings or trees. I've read that the protected area will be around 30 times the height of the feature, so a 3m marina wall will give some shelter for a distance of 90m on its downwind side. The effect diminishes gradually, but in practice this seems a fairly good guideline. If there's a strong offshore wind, it's worth staying close to the shore even if there are high cliffs.

Valleys coming down to the sea can have a major effect on the wind. For one thing you'll lose the protection of the higher shoreline. A funnel-shaped valley will concentrate the wind. If an offshore wind blows down a valley that curves off before reaching the sea, anyone paddling along the shore will suddenly encounter a surprisingly strong head or tail wind. If an unexpected breeze briefly helps you, bear in mind it could make coming back the opposite way a tough test of technique and stamina.

*Look out for valleys meeting the coast.*

# Rain

Precipitation or thawing snow in the days preceding a paddle will make the flow faster in rivers, cool the temperature and could affect the water clarity. One upside is that shallow sections may be deeper, making them easier to paddle, especially downstream, if not too fast.

When there's been a fair amount of rain, but not just after a sudden surge, rivers can be good places for a paddle. If you're suitably protected from the cold, particularly your feet, a crisp winter's day on rivers can be beautiful and especially good for wildlife watching if the water is clear.

If you're in a wetsuit rain isn't necessarily a problem. Would you rather be dry and bored or wet and having a good time? A hat can lessen the effects of rain, hail and sun.

Some days are just plain rainy and dull with it, but on seemingly less pluvial days look out for cumulonimbus clouds heading your way. They resemble the classic fluffy white cumulus clouds, but are taller and/or bigger with darker bases, and sometimes anvil-shaped. The showers they bring tend to be fairly brief, though can be heavier in summer and more prolonged near the sea.

Where cumulonimbus clouds are much bigger, seemingly filling a large section of the sky, and very dark below with ragged bases, they can produce storms. When you see these moving in your direction with grey streaks coming from the base it's probably time to call it a day.

This is particularly true if lightning ensues. The number of seconds between a flash and the sound of thunder, divided by 3, gives the approximate distance you are from the lightning in km (e.g. 6 seconds for 2km away). It may be time to upgrade from that metal paddle! Most adjustable paddles have metal in the clips, which could act as a lightning conductor and send the electric current through you.

*Blue sky thinking, cumulus clouds over Sandbanks beach.*

*Cumulonimbus cloud.*

If lightning looks likely, prone paddle and skedaddle!

## TOP TIP

If there's a likelihood of lightning, place your paddle down, lie on your board and swim for shore. In a group it's best to leave gaps of at least 5m between you. Exit the water and find shelter, but not under individual trees. It is safe to touch (and carry out first aid on) someone who's been struck.

# Sunshine

Generally sunshine is a wonderful thing when paddling and SUP is a great way to make the most of it. It's particularly good to get some vitamin D and warmth in winter. Unless you have effective sunglasses that you aren't going to lose and don't get steamed up, it is worth planning and timing your paddles so the Sun and its reflection aren't directly in view for any length of time. There are sunglasses designed for watersports with straps to hold them in place. Brimmed or peaked hats help but won't block the sun when it is very low, or its reflection. Long-term exposure to bright sunlight can cause cataracts and cloudy vision.

Obviously in summer when the sun is strong and you're in its full force, plus that reflected off the water, take suitable precautions with your skin, including waterproof sun cream. If you're having too much fun in the sun to apply protection and you burn... don't blame it on the sunshine or the good time!

*Beware the glare.*

Tintern Abbey on the River Wye.

Look out for advection or sea mist rolling in.

# Mist and fog

These both consist of fine water droplets suspended in the air and can be regarded as cloud at ground or sea level. When visibility is less than 1km it is referred to as fog, otherwise mist. There are two common types:

**Radiation or land fog** occurs when the air cools rapidly, usually at night and in calm conditions. This is more common in autumn and winter, though it will quickly blow away if the wind picks up. In summer it will often burn off by lunchtime and the temperature will increase rapidly. This kind of fog is often found in valleys, affecting lakes and rivers, not great for the views but if not too thick and heavy it can have a magical atmospheric appearance with trees and landmarks emerging from a low blanket of mist.

**Advection or sea fog** occurs when wind carries humid air over a cooler surface. This often forms over large lakes or the sea where the wind tends to carry it inland, though it can linger for several days even when windy.

Both types of fog generally occur when humidity is high. If following a river or coast, you are unlikely to get lost but be more wary of potential hazards. It can be more of an issue when crossing a large body of water and something to consider in tour and trip planning. Take spare layers of clothing to cope with temperature changes or you may have to keep up a brisk pace.

*Mist will usually burn off in summer.*

# Forecasting

Despite huge technological advances, the weather can still be difficult to predict, especially when it is unsettled. Forecasts a few days ahead often change to some extent.

TV broadcasts give a good idea of the likely paddling conditions, but these days it's worth checking internet sources for the local picture. **The BBC Weather website** (www.bbc.co.uk/weather) provides 10-day forecasts for locations in the UK, with wind speeds given in miles per hour. I try not to paddle on the open sea if the wind is 10mph or more, though less if it's offshore. Sheltered coastal areas may be OK with up to 13mph winds depending on the direction. Rivers may be OK with over 20mph winds as long as they're not blowing downstream when you need to head upstream.

**The Met Office website** (www.metoffice. gov.uk) also gives descriptions and helpful

## THE BEAUFORT SCALE

The Beaufort Scale, which features on shipping forecasts, classifies the effects of wind speeds. Francis Beaufort devised the scale in 1805. I've added the last column, though to some extent it depends on your experience and ability, as well as the wind direction and topography. A sheltered river valley may be surprisingly calm in a force 6 if you're protected from it.

| Force | Speed (knots) | Description | Offshore sea state | Wave height (m) | Paddle potential |
|-------|---------------|-------------|--------------------|-----------------| -----------------|
| 0 | <1 | Calm | Like a mirror | - | Anywhere |
| 1 | 1-3 | Light air | Rippled like scales | 0.1 | Anywhere |
| 2 | 4-6 | Light breeze | Small wavelets | 0.2 | Anywhere, though not if exposed to offshore wind |
| 3 | 7-10 | Gentle breeze | Large wavelets, hints of white horses | 0.6 | Sheltered coasts, not on open sea |
| 4 | 11-16 | Moderate breeze | Small waves, some white horses | 1.0 | Very sheltered coasts or inland |
| 5 | 17-21 | Fresh breeze | Many white horses, some spray | 2.0 | Sheltered inland |
| 6-11 | 22-63 | Strong breeze to violent storm | Large, high waves | 3.0-11.3 | No SUP |
| 12 | 64+ | Hurricane | Air filled with foam and spray | 14 | Obviously no SUP |

figures for your location for the week ahead, with wind speed (mph), gust speed, visibility and humidity. XC Weather (www.xcweather.co.uk) gives clear figures for local forecasts including wind speed averages and gusts in mph, cloud cover and air pressure.

**The Windguru website** (www.windguru.cz) was developed specially for watersports reliant on wind, such as windsurfing and kitesurfing but is very useful to Suppers too. The wind speeds are given in knots. 1 knot = 1.15mph, roughly speaking 7 knots = 8mph, 13 knots = 15mph and 20 knots = 23mph. It also gives the speed of wind gusts, which are what can knock you off balance and your board, particularly when you're on top of a wave. Often the gusts are only up to 40% higher than the general wind speed but they can be 80% faster or more, so well worth a check for sea paddles.

**Bigsalty** (www.bigsalty.com) is another watersport website with weather forecasts. For a greater understanding of weather phenomena Mailasail's Weather Window (www.weather.mailasail.com) gives excellent explanations particularly aimed at sailors. If you're heading for a surf beach, Magic Seaweed (www.magicseaweed.com) is a good specialist website to

*Waves lose choppiness and become concentric swell in the shelter of Lulworth Cove.*

check, with wave heights as well as live webcams that show what the waves are doing. Wind speeds are in mph.

**The Irish Meteorological Service** provides online forecasts on www.met.ie

www.yr.no is a **Norwegian website,** but it will also give a quick useful forecast for anywhere around the British Isles, including Ireland.

Some hotels also provide webcams, which are very helpful. It is very disappointing to pack all your stuff and drive to a location only to enter thick mist just as you arrive or find choppier waves than the figures seemed to suggest.

Radio forecasts are also useful, with more localised ones on local stations. The Shipping Forecasts given on Radio 4 (long wave) at midday and just before 6pm are useful for the sea. The last word or description for each area is the visibility, preferably 'Good'.

*Always check the forecast and plan and pack accordingly.*

# Reading the sky

People have always tried to predict the weather. Our ancestors may have lacked our technology but were probably more in tune with the elements than many of us are today, with the exception of people who work on the land or the sea, or spend much time outdoors. Seeing bees and other insects flying, and hearing plenty of birdsong or seeing sea birds on or above the water, are promising signs, as is a good dew fall.

The old saying 'Red sky at night, shepherds' delight. Red sky in the morning, shepherds' warning', appears in Matthew in the New Testament and generally it holds true. Due to the Earth's orbit and the Coriolis effect, most weather systems come from the west. High pressure, which brings settled weather, traps dust and small particles in the atmosphere. This scatters blue light leaving the red light to colour the sky. If red skies appear in the evening they will be coming our way from the west. Appearing in the east in the morning may mean they've already gone past.

Clouds can also give an indication, but sometimes similar looking or closely related cloud formations can lead to different conditions. Massive grey

Red skies in the evening and billows usually mean good weather coming.

nimbostratus clouds are obviously rainy. As mentioned, cumulonimbus clouds or frontal clouds arranged at 45° can bring showers or thunder, especially if there's a sudden drop in temperature.

Clouds that resemble the pattern on a mackerel could be billows, which are a sign of settled weather. However, altocumulus clouds can have a fairly similar pattern, but tend to bring rain within 12 hours or thunder within 24 hours. Sets of cirrus clouds occurring high in the sky are sometimes called mares' tails due to their wispy appearance. Generally they mean fair weather for the moment, but if cloud cover increases storms could follow.

A sneaky, scientifically backed weather forecasting trick is based on

Paddling above the clouds.

Facing the wind, dark clouds to the right will head your way.

a rule known as the Buys Ballot Law. It is named after a Dutch meteorologist who published it back in 1857. It states that if you stand with your back to the wind in the Northern Hemisphere, low pressure systems will come in from the left moving anticlockwise and high pressure systems come from the right. The opposite is true in the Southern Hemisphere.

To put this in practice, stand with your back to the wind. If looking over sea, turn 10 degrees to your right or if over land turn 20 degrees right. This adjustment is to do with the effect of friction on the wind and this being greater on land.

Now look up at the sky. If the clouds are moving from left to right it means low pressure is the dominant force in your location and the weather is, or will tend to become, less settled. If the clouds are moving from the right it means high pressure and settled weather.

If you see a storm cloud coming, face into the wind and turn very slightly to the right again. If the sky is dark grey/black on your right or straight in front it will be heading your way. If it is to the left as you look up it will pass you. This is fun to try, particularly if it suggests the cloud will miss you!

Visible vapour trails from planes are also a sign of good weather.

Altocumulus tend to bring rain.

# Climate change

When it comes to climate and climate change, it isn't hard to perceive an ominous elephant in the room, with the prospect of drought and deluge, doom and gloom, looming not far away. Any problems to watersport enthusiasts pale into insignificance compared to those whose lives are devastated by hurricanes, floods, sea level rise or coastal erosion, or those displaced by desertification or wild fires.

*Flood damaged fences can prove hazardous, especially for inflatables.*

Warm air rising off the sea will generate more frequent storms with greater violence and more prolonged spells of wild, unsettled, 'unsuppable' weather. Periods of intense drought and heat will dry up lakes and rivers in some areas, particularly as there will be more water abstraction from rivers. With less water to dilute pollutants, filamentous alga (blanket weed) will choke more of these watercourses. Gravel pit lakes will continue to be created and more reservoirs will be needed. Winters could be wetter, and areas that already receive much rainfall could see an increase.

This could threaten dams, as happened at Whaley Bridge in Derbyshire.

Although generally rivers will be lower in water and shorter in length, more intense downpours at times will lead to more erosion and thus more sediment in our rivers, as well as pollution and in some places damaged barbed wire fences. Waste water treatment plants may struggle to cope in these conditions, meaning more sewage in our rivers and ultimately the sea. There will be fewer good days for Supping, less visibility, less water clarity and more chance of becoming ill, particularly if you fall in. Paddlers may consider joining the campaigns of 'Surfers Against Sewage' (www.sas.org.uk).

'Seasons out of time' will be no joy and fun for wildlife whose food supply is affected. Shelled creatures need alkaline calcium carbonate. Higher acidity means they can't produce healthy shells. With less shelled wildlife to use up carbon the problem becomes worse. One group of creatures that seem to cope with a slight increase in acidity is jellyfish. They will be encountered by Suppers more often, but as they prosper it will upset the delicate balance of sea life.

*Tipping point: no matter how you look at it, some positions are unsustainable.*

The age of precarious. Paddling through ice in Kenai Fjords National Park, Alaska.

The more adaptable will cope but the more specialist and rarer species will suffer and may become extinct.

Small reasonable considerations and choices may seem like the tip of the iceberg, literally, but can combine to make a difference. For example, sticking to ecofriendly dishwasher tablets or washing up by hand will apparently be a big help to the health of our rivers.

At least paddleboarding itself is green and anything that helps us to appreciate the environment encourages us to tread lightly on the planet. Obviously with most pastimes there can be travel issues, though Suppers tend to car share where practical. Not needing roof racks for inflatable boards means more efficient fuel use, though a roof rack may mean more people can car share.

Paddleboarding in far flung places can broaden our understanding of life on Earth, so it's a shame it can also damage it. Some airlines invite passengers to make a small contribution to offset their carbon footprint. There's plenty of potential for paddleboarders to play their part in paddling to protect the planet.

Baby on board.

# 8 SENSE OF ADVENTURE!

# Tour planning

It may be best to stick to the rivers and the lakes that you're used to at first, but there may come a time when you would like to plan voyages of discovery! This will bring a great sense of purpose, adventure and satisfaction to your paddling. Before thinking that the ocean's your oyster and embarking on an expedition, a certain amount of thought and preparation is necessary to ensure everything goes smoothly.

## Organised tours

One of the best ways to induct yourself into the world of SUP touring is to go with a very experienced friend or join an organised trip. You could try something expected to last up to two hours, where less experienced people are welcome.

Don't go chasing waterfalls on a maiden voyage.

The emphasis may be on skills or the location or a combination.

Supping attracts sociable friendly folk and brings out the gregarious side in most people. You may want to join a group trip with a companion so you can look out for each other and give each other a congratulatory pat on the back (or shoulder massage) afterwards. Some leaders will be great at giving tips and encouragement and may have local knowledge of interest.

A tour sets out from Lulworth Cove on Dorset's Jurassic Coast.

Greek Odyssey.

8 • SENSE OF ADVENTURE!

# Plan your own paddles

You can learn a lot from organised expeditions and think how you could best plan a trip yourself. There are a couple of ways to do this:

1 **Plan a route** and wait for the right conditions.
2 **Assess the conditions** and plan a route accordingly.

If you've done number 1 for several locations, you'll be in a better 'place' to use number 2. Think about the following checklist of questions:

1 **What are the weather conditions,** including wind and visibility? Are there any changes forecast?
2 **For a river,** how much rain has there been and what will the flow be like?
3 **For tidal paddles,** what will the tide be doing?
4 **Who is going?**

Think about ability and pace. You can only go as fast or as far as the slowest/least able people in your group can cope with. This may not be fully known or equipment could be a factor. You may be able to encourage and help people, with skills like parallel paddling, but you need to make allowances in your plans with ways to shorten a trip if necessary. You don't want anyone to feel too stretched/pressured or for the group to spread out too much. Look out for the less proficient paddlers, particularly if the going gets tough. Most experienced Suppers can paddle at good walking pace or faster.

Having narrowed potential options down, think about:

- How long will it take?
- What time and where to meet?
- How will you get there and back with everyone and your equipment?
- Are there any accessible places to stop in case there's a problem?
- Who to inform of your plans and whether you can contact them?
- What to take, including food and drink?

*If you're well matched with good equipment you can cover long distances.*

# Fine tuning

Generally you would plan a route that is easier on the way back or toward the end, when you may well be tired, for instance head upstream or into the wind to begin with. There can be exceptions, such as if the tide changes or on a gently flowing river so you avoid having the sun in your eyes so much.

*Plan with the tide for an easy ride!*

Details can be important:

- Which route is more sheltered from the wind? For example you may want to stick to one side of an estuary to avoid a cross-wind.
- On the way out along the coast, you may want to tuck into a coastal bay to gain some protection but head straight past on your return, with the wind behind you.
- The shape of an island, combined with the wind and tide, should be considered when deciding which way round to circumnavigate it.
- If the tide is due to change, do you want to have it slightly in your favour both ways? It may be easier overall to paddle into a fairly slack tide on the way out but, by the rule of twelfths, come back with a good tide helping you. You may be able to have a break, possibly for food, while the tide changes or increases.
- Timing on tidal rivers can be crucial, but remember upstream from the sea there will be a delay so allow for tides acting later than the tables.
- If crossing a large body of water like a lake or harbour, which way will make

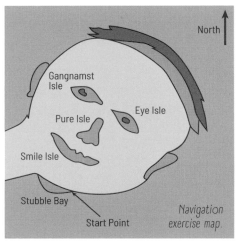
*Navigation exercise map.*

navigation easier? Prominent features are easier to head for and coming back the visibility may deteriorate.

The map above shows a large bay. If it was within a very large lake, which route would you take from Start Point to go around Smile Isle and return to Start Point? You can take any route you like as long as you've completely gone around Smile Isle.

**Plan your route if the wind was blowing from:**

1 West; 2 North; 3 East; 4 South.

Navigation exercise route suggestions.

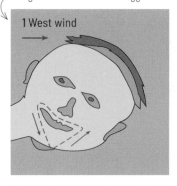

1 West wind

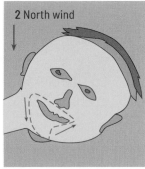

2 North wind

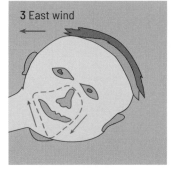

3 East wind

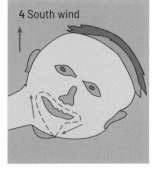

4 South wind

Which direction would make for the easiest journey?

If the bay was coastal and tidal, linked to the open sea on the west side, this would be another major factor to consider. Your choice would depend on the relative strengths of the wind and tide. Ideally you would time your paddle so the tide helped you, particularly on the way back.

You wouldn't plan a route where both tide and wind were against you for the last leg of your journey.

When you arrive at your start point, see whether the conditions meet your expectations. One way you can tell whether the dominant factor is the wind or the tide/current is to look at anchored boats. Their fronts will point into the direction of the strongest factor as they are pulled away from their anchors. Paddling will be easiest in the opposite direction to the one they face. Sometimes boats in one part of a harbour will point a different way to those not far away, indicating where there's more shelter or current. You may be able to use this to your advantage.

Bear in mind that deep-keeled yachts may be more affected by tidal currents, whereas speedboats that float on the surface, displacing little water, may be comparatively more wind-affected. If you can see lines coming from watercraft,

A change in water texture can indicate water flowing in different directions.

Boats point into the dominant factor.

they will be pulled taut by strong effects. Buoys will also be pulled by currents and attached seaweed will give added evidence of the influence of flows. Modify your plans if required.

Here are suggestions for good routes in the exercise:

Suggestions:

1 **West** – anticlockwise.

2 **North** – anticlockwise sheltering from wind and coming back with it helping (probably the easiest wind direction here).

3 **East** – clockwise; it would be longer but may be easier to go around Pure Isle too with shelter from Eye Isle.

4 **South** – clockwise; slightly harder than North as you will encounter some wind at the end when you may be tired.

Adjust your routes to take shelter from the wind provided by landform, trees or buildings.

# What to pack

This may vary depending on the location, the conditions, your plans and your group, but should often include:

- Buoyancy aid.
- Dry-bag.
- First aid kit with head bandage and tick remover.
- Drinking water.
- Spare clothing and warm hat.
- Mobile phone or means of communication.
- Money.
- Small waterproof case for phone/keys/money.
- Head-torch.
- Knife with saw blade and blunt end, in holder.
- Food.
- Map, compass and pencil.
- Whistle.
- Your emergency contact details in case you're found unconscious, for example.

Dry-bags are very useful to store these items. The tops roll up to form a watertight

seal and they have clips to attach to your board strings or handle. Diver's or canoeist's knives have blunt ends and come in a protective sheath. They have one sharp side and one serrated, which can be useful amid the tangled challenge of a narrow well-vegetated river.

*Take a SUP on the wild side!*

You could also include:

- Spare leash.
- Throw bag or throw line.
- Foil blanket.
- Towel.
- Spare sectioned paddle if going a long way with a group.
- Footwear.
- Cagoule.
- Bite cream and insect repellant.
- Sun cream.
- Flare.
- A watch, possibly one providing information such as distances eg. a Garmin.
- Camera.
- Repair kit.
- Snorkel/mask.
- Hot drink.
- Picnic.
- Lashings of ginger beer, which can prevent seasickness (optional and, of course, not lashings if alcoholic!).

A throw bag is a rope packed in and attached to a handy bag, available from watersports retailers. If someone is in difficulty, perhaps on a tricky bit of river, you can hold the end of the rope firmly and throw the bag to them. If they can grab the bag, you can pull them to safety. It takes a little practice to throw accurately, ideally just to the upstream side of them. Unfortunately repacking the bag can take a couple of minutes, as you need to feed it in rather than stuffing it. If you pull the rope back in neat arm length loops, you can repeat throwing without repacking if required.

With clear, biodiverse water a snorkel and mask can add interest either for

snorkeling or simply lying on your board and looking over the side. Looking over the very front isn't advisable as the board will probably tilt and dunk you. Leaving your leash on will help keep you and your board safe, though could be limiting.

It can be useful to take a trug (large bucket) in your vehicle, particularly for wet items after a paddle. An old towel can be useful to wipe kit down and you could line your car boot with an old sheet. Obviously the longer the trip the more equipment, food and drink you'll have to pack, plus overnight requirements if planned or possibly needed. Whatever you take to eat, take what you need to eat it with.

*See the sea below your SUP.*

# Navigation

Many trips don't take the navigational skill of Captain Cook; you can just follow the shoreline or river and remember the features of the landscape so you recognise where to finish. If you're crossing open water, such as a large lake, bay, harbour or a stretch of sea it may be more challenging. This is particularly true if mist or bad weather occur or the light fades on an evening paddle, though there are ways to help demystify the challenge of finding your way. You may rarely need navigation skills, but when you do they can be crucial.

Building up your skills in good conditions may prove invaluable, especially if you're planning or leading adventurous expeditions. Outdoor centres with access to large bodies

*Don't lose yourself in a sunset, or after it!*

of water can set up something like an orienteering course or treasure trail using buoyed markers.

These days GPS systems can make navigating a lot easier. They're generally reliable and can give useful information such as your location. They can help you to follow a pre-planned route marked with waypoints (points along your route) and tell you how far you are from them as well as your 'cross track error' (how much you're drifting off course). There are, however, more traditional, reliable techniques and you may prefer to trust these and your own instincts and judgement. The more you practise these, the greater your understanding will become and the more prepared you'll be if you don't have the use of GPS.

Always try to be reasonably aware of where you are. Maps or charts are invaluable. The more detailed the scale the better, so with Ordnance Survey maps, a scale of 1:25,000 will be far better than 1:50,000. Charts, such as those produced by Imray or Stanfords, tend to be an even better scale, with more detailed information about the sea including the direction and strength of tidal flows. Maps show more land features. Landmarks are well worth observing, especially if you can line up two, such as a small headland with a building or a hill on the horizon. Admiralty Tidal Stream Atlases are very useful around islands and other prominent coastal features to show how the tidal currents behave from hour to hour.

The other time-honoured tool is a compass. There are different types but a basic hiker's compass will be very useful. If you know how to use one along with a few navigational techniques, you'll be a lot safer. As a paddleboarder you may want to have this on a string that could fit around your neck, though it can go in your dry-bag or buoyancy aid pocket when not needed. Ideally you would set it up, as

*Some people tape a section of chart or a print out from Google Earth to their boards.*

described below, from a steady position, ideally the shore. If not go to your knees. You may be able to find a buoy to attach your leash to or a boat to shelter by.

Using a compass to work out which direction to take:

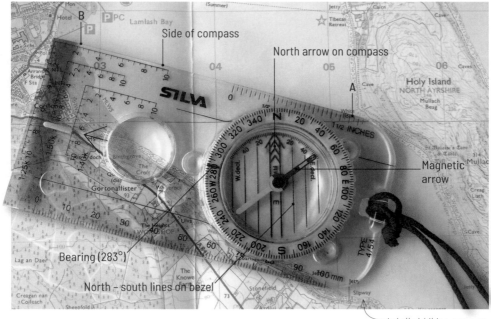

*Labelled hiking compass.*

**1** **Line up the side** of your compass from where you are on the map to where you want to go (A to B) with the arrow on the base of the compass pointing in the direction of travel.

**2** **Line up the north-south lines** on the compass dial (known as a 'bezel') parallel to the grid lines on the map, with north uppermost (getting these the wrong way up is a common mistake!).

**3** **Take the compass off** the map and read the bearing (283° in the example shown). You will have to turn the dial to make a slight adjustment based on magnetic variation. Don't worry about this for now, it will be described below. (Tip: You should have a rough idea of which direction you should head. If the bearing is pointing in the opposite direction to what you expected, check you haven't made the common mistake above.)

**4** **Line up the magnetic arrow** on the compass with the north arrow on the bezel and head in the direction of the arrow on the compass base.

If you can see something to aim for such as a buoy or a feature on the shore this will save much looking down at the compass, which isn't good for balance. Don't pick something that is likely to move, such as a floating bird! If you have no landmark, you will be less affected by the wind on your knees. With waves, currents, wind and having to swap paddle sides, it can be difficult to maintain the same direction. If one person goes a little way ahead within easy earshot you may get some idea of how well they are following the direction and can correct accordingly.

Unfortunately, there is a variation between Magnetic North and True North so you must read the number of degrees that the base arrow points from and adjust this slightly. The amount of adjustment in your location is worth knowing and can be found on the website www.magnetic-declination.com

At the time of writing these are, in the UK for example, 0° in eastern England, around -1° from the Midlands to the Welsh border, -2° in West Wales and -4° in West Ireland, while Scotland ranges from -1° in the east to -3° in the west. These change by a fraction of a degree each year, so are worth checking. Currently, if the bearing of a landmark reads 70° on the compass on the east coast of Scotland it should be 70 – 1 = 69°.

In the example shown previously of 283°, as Holy Island is off the Isle of Arran on Scotland's west coast, this would become 283 – 3 = 280°. So give the dial a slight clockwise twist to line up the arrow on the base with 280°.

As the compass diagram shows, if the journey is a long one, the side of the compass may be too short. If pre-planning a long stretch you can use a ruler with the compass or a device known as a 'plotter', which resembles a large compass.

Imagine you're situated at the end of Sea Spray Spit on the map opposite and want to paddle to a car park between Mute Point and Tipping Point. Various techniques could help you. They may not be the shortest route, but they could involve less time, effort and certainly less concern than becoming disorientated. They will require a map or chart of your area and some will involve a compass. **What route would you try in poor visibility?**

1 If there's a moderate or strong westerly.
2 If there's very little wind.
3 If there's a light easterly.

Here are some popular navigational strategies you could deploy:

- **Hand-railing** – one of the simplest techniques, which doesn't require a compass, is called 'hand-railing'. On land this will involve tracking along a feature shown on your map, such as a stream or field boundary. On water this would mean following the shore, possibly crossing a few small bays where you can see the other side. This is very reliable, but if you're tired, the light's fading or you're pushed for time, it might not be the best way as other routes require less paddling.
- **Aiming off** – rather than setting your compass for your destination and heading straight for it, there is merit in aiming to one side of it, especially if your end point isn't very obvious. This way when you reach the shore you know which way

you must turn to find where you're going to. On land, you may only need to aim 5° off, maybe 10° if it's windy, to be sure of which way you must turn. As this is much harder on water, it may be better to aim off by at least 10° if calm and 20° if windy. It needn't be so necessary if you're very familiar with the shoreline.

- **Attack point** – there may be an obvious place, perhaps a large rock, very small island or headland shown on the chart/ map that would be easier to find than your destination. If so, it may be best to head for that first, particularly if it's roughly en route. Think big: the larger the target, the simpler finding it will be. Having found this 'attack point', it will then be easier to head to and find your destination.

Aiming directly for the car park you could end up at Mist, Mute or Tipping Point. In poor visibility you wouldn't know which one so you wouldn't know which way to turn. It may be a little while before you were sure whether you'd headed in

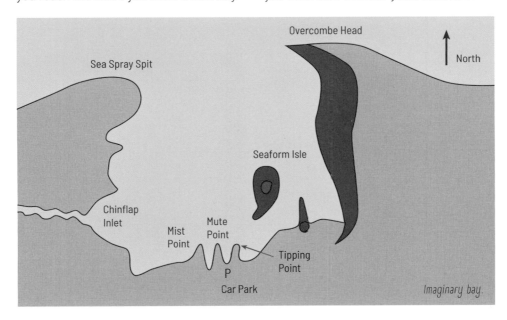

Imaginary bay.

the wrong direction. If you were going from Sea Spray Spit to Overcombe Head instead, missing would be more serious. This shows why it is a good idea to know what your normal pace would be in different conditions. You can work this out from using maps and timing yourself or using an app like Strava. If you were expecting to reach Overcombe Head in 15 minutes you would at least know to head left/south if there was no sign of land after 18 minutes (20% over).

If there was a fair wind from the west, hand-railing around the coast would give you protection from the wind and should get you to the car park OK (red route on map). You could cut across small mini-bays to some extent, particularly if the other side was visible. Take care across Chinflap Inlet as there may be a current taking you out of this small bay. You wouldn't need a compass, but it would be helpful to follow a map.

With little wind, a fairly efficient strategy would be to aim for the centre of the island as an attack point on a compass bearing (purple line on map).

From the southern corner of Seaform Isle, you could then aim slightly to the west of Tipping Point and find the car park. If you had missed the island you would at least know to head west along the shore to find the car park.

With a light easterly, you could aim off around 5° to the west of Mist Point (green route on map). Given the wind direction, you would be unlikely to head too far east. Once you reach the shore, head east to find the car park, missing out the mini-bay between Mist and Mute Points. If you were travelling from the spit to Overcombe Head, aiming off south would generally be your best strategy, allowing more room for error depending on the wind strength and direction.

What if you don't know your location, particularly if you're in open water?

As mentioned, if you can see two landmarks you can use these on a map to get a good idea of your location. This is known as a 'transit' and without needing to use a compass you can imagine or draw a pencil line going through the landmarks on your map to narrow down your position.

*Better to aim for a small island than a bird.*

*Kneel down to take your bearing.*

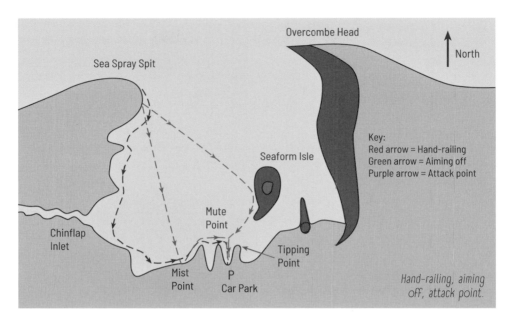

Overcombe Head

North

Sea Spray Spit

Key:
Red arrow = Hand-railing
Green arrow = Aiming off
Purple arrow = Attack point

Seaform Isle

Chinflap
Inlet

Mute
Point

Tipping
Point

Mist
Point

P
Car Park

*Hand-railing, aiming
off, attack point.*

You can find out the direction of landmarks with a compass. The procedure is the reverse of taking a bearing from a map. If you then draw pencil lines from landmarks on your map, where lines from two landmarks meet will give a good approximation of your location.

With three landmarks there is less chance of making an error. The process is known as 'triangulation'. The lines will form a triangle and your best estimate of your location will be in the middle, equidistant from the corners of the triangle. If one is a 'transit', it will help. The more spread out the directions the better. If the visibility is poor but you have a rough idea of the direction of three landmarks you can estimate your location this way.

If you're moving with the wind or currents this is likely to make the process less accurate. In some places magnetic properties in local geology will cause distortions in the magnetic field. Off Australia, between Townsville and the Barrier Reef lies Magnetic Island, so

named because of the effect it had on Captain Cook's ship's compass.

You should always have a reasonable idea of where you are and what direction will get you to the shore. Some kayaks have a compass fitted in front of the paddler. Taping one to your deck could help you to stay aware of your location. Launching the Compass app on an iPhone will enable you to head in roughly the right direction. Assuming the sun isn't visible, which would be useful, the wind direction may give a clue, but be alert to any changes. If this fails you could try a flare if you have one or will have to call the Coastguard in a genuine time of need.

1 **Dial 999** (UK) or 112 (International) and ask for Coastguard.

2 **Describe your location** (as best you can).

3 **Describe your group** (number of people/boards).

4 **Describe your problem** and any additional information.

Keep calm and stay together if lost. Any route that may involve tricky navigation would be best done with at least three people. On a positive note, finding your way after becoming lost is apparently a good way to stimulate new connections in the brain.

## TOP TIP

..........................

Memory aid: PORT has the same number of letters as LEFT and the same colour as the drink port, which people might feel like they need after coming back into port.

## What do buoys mean?

Buoys may be useful to head for in navigation but their positions on charts may be out of date. They are regulated by the International Association of Lighthouse Authorities and are sometimes added, moved or removed. There are different types and it's worth knowing what they signify.

Lateral marks show the sides of a channel for ships/boats coming into a port, harbour or estuary. These are red on the port (left) side and vary in form, usually being a can shape or with a can shape on top. On the starboard (right) side they are green with a cone shape. The centre-line at the start of a channel may have a red and white striped buoy.

In America and around the Pacific Rim they are the opposite way around: red on the port side as you leave the port. In Scandinavia, 'finger posts' like country road markers mark minor channels.

Where there is a preferred channel, as opposed to a clearly defined one, these will have a horizontal stripe of the opposite colour but the rest of them will be the usual colour and shape.

As a Supper you won't normally be sticking to a shipping channel, you'll be trying to avoid them. At least you'll know where to look out for boats.

*As you come in: red can to the left/port; green cone to the right/starboard.*

Size matters; watch for the wake. You could shelter behind a moored boat.

If crossing shipping lanes, assemble as a group, possibly by a buoy or boat. Agree a place to head for, ideally straight across to keep to the shortest route. Kneeling is advisable, especially if the water is busy or choppy. Look and listen in all directions. You should find out first if any major ferries are scheduled. A small boat should make way for you

Beware shipping lanes even on a megaSup (especially on a megaSup!).

but a tanker has right of way and would struggle! Maintain a good pace but stay together, so the slowest person dictates that pace. Reassemble once across to check everyone is alright. Wear and turn on head-torches if visibility isn't good.

Cardinal marks are yellow and black, like a wasp's warning colours, and show hazards to boats, which might not necessarily be a problem to SUPs but are worth being aware of. They will indicate one of the cardinal points of the compass, by means of two triangles on top of them as on the following page:

Cardinal mark buoy indicating a hazard to the east of it.

**If both triangles point upward**
the cardinal buoy will be situated to the north of a hazard with clear water to the north of it. Up for north, as on a map, should be easily remembered.

**Both triangles point down**
if the buoy is to the south of the hazard.

**They point toward each other**
(like a diablo) if the buoy is to the west of the hazard.

**They point opposite each other,**
with the upper one up and the lower one down, with a line/gap in the middle if the buoy is to the east of the hazard.

Some buoys mark zones for certain activities.

Cardinal buoy south.

In the above photo the mark shown will be to the south of the hazard.

Other buoys may mark zoned areas for swimmers, water-skiers, yacht races or for military exercises. Some small ones may simply be mooring buoys. Others may be labelled to show features or speed limits: the latter don't tend to apply to Suppers!

Lateral mark for right side of channel.

# Down-winders and down-streamers

If there are two or more of you with transport, a good route option may be to paddle in one direction, without paddling back to your start point. This is possible on your own if you have a reliable means of getting back. The advantages of one way paddles are that you can:

- Have the elements (wind, tide, flow) in your favour the whole way.
- Go on slightly windier days or when there's faster river flow.
- Travel more than twice as far.

The proviso is that it requires careful planning to ensure you have vehicles capable of carrying all your equipment at both ends of the journey. Look after your car keys! There may be other options that involve less waiting and ferrying.

If you're travelling further, with a few of you, it may be worth having one vehicle parked along the route if there's a suitable access point, just in case. People waiting could be pumping up inflatable boards. At least one person will need a good logical mind!

You may need to pick a day/time when the forecast is sufficiently settled that the wind is unlikely to change and become a problem. If you're travelling quickly downriver, be very careful not to get caught or snagged as it may be impossible for others to get back to help you:

- Stay together.
- Communicate/warn each other about obstacles.
- Wait for each other as soon as you can.
- Take mobile phones.
- Carry blunt-ended canoeists' knives to cut yourself free.
- Don't use a long leash. One that can be easily released is best.

You'll need to be confident that all stretches are accessible. If not the flow may be too strong to return the way you came and you could be up or down the proverbial creek without a paddle. One or two people may be able to pass once, one way, through a zealously guarded fishing club area with care and, if necessary, an apology or explanation. A group, however, is more likely to evoke animosity. A generous portion of politeness costs nothing and may, literally, get you a long way.

Travelling light has an intrinsic appeal but take enough clothing, particularly on a river, as you may be cooler than you hoped going downstream the whole way.

*Bridge over the River Wye. On a wet wintery day downstream is the only way.*

# Night paddling

It's well worth thinking outside the box when you plan the time of your paddles. Try a late evening paddle and see how it awakens your senses, especially if you're not used to such manoeuvres in the dark. Feeling the cool night air on your face is a good antidote to a day in a stuffy office.

Supping as the sun slides into the water ahead of you is a magical way to feel more involved in a sunset than with any land-based activity. Embrace this everyday occurrence and turn it into a beautiful, inspiring and memorable experience.

A sunrise paddle, possibly before work, can put you in an uplifted mood for the rest of the day. Some friends of mine made the effort to paddle at dawn along what is later a busy stretch of Poole's main beach and were rewarded by seeing a small pod of dolphins.

*Celebrate Supping late.*

Supping in the dark can add an extra dimension to the excitement of an adventure. You'll want good conditions and extra clothing. At sea or on a navigable inland waterway, you'll need to be seen. Head-torches and high-visibility clothing are pretty much essential, though glow-sticks are helpful, fun and

*The golden hour.*

won't completely ruin your night vision. These provisions are sometimes worth taking in daylight, in case of fog.

On a river without boat traffic it would be advisable to take head-torches, though you may have a more enchanting experience by relying on your own night vision and heightened other senses. Either way it's worth knowing the area well and checking it out in daylight first. That barbed wire or rusty pipe won't be as obvious in the dark.

Wildlife encounters could be more of a thrill, though try to remain calm if a curious seal surfaces beside you. Otters will be more active and deer on the saltmarshes may venture closer to the shore. Swans are still easy to see and can be surprisingly busy after dark.

You may also see bats patrolling their flight paths. Pipistrelles are reasonably common and Daubenton's bats are known as the water bat, as they specialise in hunting over it. If you're under 30 you may hear their whistles. Appreciate this before your hearing range contracts! They use these sounds to echo-locate, so they won't collide with you, but can pinpoint mosquitoes and midges as well as crunching through their favourite food of moths. Daubenton's are on average almost twice as heavy as the smaller pipistrelle, though they can both add another 50% to their mass after a good night's feeding.

Be safe, be seen, go with a glow.

When navigating in darkness, lights may make it easier to find some well-lit features or destinations. On a clear night, a brilliant aid to finding your way in the Northern Hemisphere is the North Star. To locate this find the seven stars that make up the Plough. Think of this as a saucepan shape, then find the two stars that make up the side of the pan furthest from the handle. Imagine a line leading up from the one at the base of the pan, through the other one then in the same line through the sky until you reach a bright star. This is the North Star or Polaris and it will always be pretty much due north from you. The entire sky appears to rotate around Polaris due to the Earth's rotation, so the Plough asterism can be at any orientation, not just at the one shown in the picture.

*Carried away by a moonlight paddle.*

*Polaris (far left) and the Plough.*

*Summer evening river paddle.*

# Supping through the seasons

Summer is clearly a wonderful time to paddle, with warm water, warm air and long evenings. Many of the taller waterside flowers are at their best. On very hot days, rivers can be even warmer than the sea, but both are still great to cool off in. You often won't need a wetsuit, depending on the conditions, so the water is the best place to be. After many people's working day there's still plenty of time to enjoy a paddle and watch the sunset. In some inland areas there can be a few blood-hungry insects about, but it's wonderful to watch jumping fish catching the biting blighters.

As a well-known sign that summer is here, swallows migrate to Europe from South Africa and use their exemplary flying skills to rid us of more mosquitoes. Suppers are well placed to observe their aerobatics as they swerve around us, though their numbers are dwindling. You may also witness them collect clay in their mouths from riverbanks and ponds in order to make their nests in outbuildings.

As the leaves become a predictable riot of countless colours, paddling is a great way to appreciate autumn, particularly inland, but also as you look from sea to shore. The water is still warm in the sea, though as the weeks go on you'll want footwear inland. Supping is a good way to make the most of the waning evening light as sunsets enhance the glowing hues of the leaves.

For beautiful quiet paddles, sunny winter days can be stunning, though this is the wetsuit season and you'll want neoprene footwear as the water may be very cold. Clear skies can mean especially chilly mornings, though at least you don't have to set your alarm too early for a sunrise paddle. Be aware of the faster flows on rivers with more rainfall sometimes combined with snow melting upstream. A downstream paddle may be the best option. The golden stems and

*Autumn hues on Loch Ederline, Argyll, Scotland.*

downy seed heads of reeds brighten up the route, while the lack of leaves allows more light in and longer views across the valleys.

In some areas there may be more birds having a break from the harsher winters of Iceland or Scandinavia. It's a great time to have the occasional paddle fix, a dose of vitamin D and lift any winter blues.

Exercising in cold conditions increases blood flow to the brain, which has an anti-ageing benefit.

Really cold clear days can be particularly beautiful on inland water, though if you see a few lines forming on the surface, try not to become trapped by ice! It is possible to bust through before it sets hard. In a group, deciding who has the toughest board or cheapest paddle could be a good way to break the ice!

In spring the water will be cool so you may still want to be suited and booted in neoprene. The lengthening evenings and warming air temperatures, along with blossoming bushes and budding trees, are bound to fill you with optimism for the

*Snowy Baltic inlet, Edsviken, near Stockholm, Sweden.*

good weather ahead. Generally wildlife is becoming more active and the birdsong on inland waters reaches its peak. Calm freshwater options mean you're less likely to fall in if you're new to paddling. If you're fairly accomplished, it's like riding a bike: you shouldn't forget how, even if you've had a winter break, and you may want to sharpen your reflexes with a few waves.

A great place to appreciate some of the seasons is the Lake District. With many broad-leaved woodlands adjoining the waters, autumn is awash with warm colours, before dropping temperatures bring icing on the lakes and snow becomes the icing on the cake of Lakeland mountain views. The woodlands also leave enough light and room for blooming beautiful spring flowers. May, June and then September are often blessed with much sunshine here.

*The first warm days of spring are a good chance to peel off the wetsuit.*

July and August bring crowds, clouds and their convectional rainfall, so for me the sunny, south coasts of Dorset and Devon trump the Cumbrian summer.

*Watch out for ice forming.*

# Photography

One of the relatively early purposes attributed to paddleboarding was to enable Hawaiian 'beach boy' surf instructors to capture images of their clients in action. Given that amid the waves they had to look down into 'Box Brownie' cameras this is a real testament to their skill and balance.

Nowadays we are blessed with compact, robust waterproof cameras that can be slipped around the neck or into a buoyancy aid pocket, ideally with a float attached. Many photos taken from SUPs are captured with mobile phones. Although a few phones are designed to be water-resistant a waterproof case is an almost essential item, though some have fiddly, easily-damaged catches. It is possible and less risky to take photos with phones from within a transparent pouch.

Phone cameras have improved greatly and are good for static shots in good light levels. They are the most handy option, with no need to carry a separate camera and there are various apps to instantly edit images before posting online. Dedicated digital cameras can capture images of higher quality, particularly with action shots. They may also have a good optical zoom. Some popular, robust waterproof cameras have a zoom of around five times, though they don't have the optical zoom often needed for shy wildlife. We also have GoPros and their like, which may be attached to a board, paddle or hand-held mount. They can take good action footage and stills from some interesting perspectives.

Given the unrivalled views we are treated to, photography is a wonderful aspect of this pastime. Views and

*A waterproof camera can capture and enrich a trip.*

spontaneous action shots, taken with fairly basic digital cameras, can be particularly pleasing from a SUP. Games and challenges evoke expressions of excitement, while race photos can capture the exertion and grit of those competing. SUP surfing usually requires a long lens. Paddling provides opportunities to closely observe and gain wonderful insights into water-based wildlife, which will help you to photograph it. That said, focusing on an eel while drifting toward a weir is an exciting challenge but unlikely to bring a good outcome.

Rivers and lakes may make for well-balanced compositions. Trees, vegetation or bridges can be used to frame the main subject, as can caves. Coastlines may have other intriguing and inspiring landforms.

The light is often striking on water especially at sunrise and sunset. Just outside these times is termed the 'Blue Hour' by photographers and inside them the 'Golden Hour', though people will look silhouetted. Lakes tend to be more tranquil then and Supping offers you beautiful mirrored reflections adding greatly to stunning scenery or the charm of autumn leaves. Rippled reflections and, at the end of the day, sunsets with cloud patterns can sometimes be even more striking than glassy calm water and unbroken blue sky. Imaginative ideas can make inspiring photos.

If you're trying to take incredible images of birds and other creatures with an SLR camera and a long lens, an open canoe may be a less hazardous option. They can even accommodate a tripod. Standing up can provide a better view, though kneeling will give more stability and less blur from wobbling. With calm

*Ripples and clouds enhance a sunset.*

169

*This balanced action shot has a certain 'X' factor!*

water, lying down will be the most stable position but that is more comfortable on an inflatable SUP than canoes or kayaks. The lower you are, the less threatening you will appear to wildlife, though don't head too close.

Supping could heighten your interest in photography and you may want more sophistication than a 'point and shoot'. With an SLR or a bridge camera, one accessory that may be worth purchasing is a circular polariser. These are particularly useful to the Supper as they cut out unwanted reflections, so much clearer underwater detail is captured. It is as though the water surface has been peeled back, allowing the camera to peer at the fascinating aquatic world below. They also reduce the effects of haze and air pollution so skies look bluer and clouds more defined. Prices vary dramatically with quality.

These days many effects can be achieved

*To avoid concerning a seal, kneel!*

*In an utterly awesome otter spot, the floating fern-look could be an option.*

with computers. Circular polarising filters enable photographers to create in-camera effects not possible after the image is taken, even with digital image editing software.

On the sea, if the going gets rough you may want to secure your camera in a dry-bag, though it won't be instantly handy. Waterproof camera housing is another option.

Unless a photo's purpose is to show how a creature looks, it may be better not to fill the frame. Showing habitat can give a sense of place and context or tell more of a story, as can including more of the direction wildlife is heading. It can make for a better composition to have the subject or a significant feature just over 60% of the way from any of the photo's four sides (known as the 'golden ratio') or roughly a third/two thirds to be simpler, rather than central. This may also be the case for placing Suppers, or cropping later.

That's the theory, though I'm just glad if I capture the subject while my board decides which way to spin around! Moving water generally adds to the challenge of taking a steady shot, with good composition and your chosen features of foreground and background perfectly aligned. The wind blowing you along or

*Here the arms of the yoga class complement and pay homage to the cranes in London's Docklands.*

turning you adds to the fun, or frustration if you miss a good shot. It's often worth taking a few in quick succession or a 'shutter-burst', for example, as the swan flies past your face.

Rivers can be particularly tricky as you mustn't lose all track of what's going on around you, where the river is taking you and potential hazards. The sea can be more exposed and subject to variable forces so watch your position and look out for boats or the possibility of being washed toward rocks.

One idea I had proved ill-considered. On a stretch of river with a fairly swift flow, I steadied myself to take a photo by hooking my arm over a tree branch on my upstream side. As I composed the shot, my board suddenly shot a few feet downstream. This left me with a branch under one arm, my primed camera in the other hand and with the outstretched toes of one foot desperately gripping my board. After a good couple of minutes of struggling, a few scratches and all the strength I could muster, I did manage to pull myself together. Sadly I never managed to take the photo that might have been a wonderful addition to this book.

A photographer wanting to really look inside the head of the subject, a bowhead whale in Khabarovsk Territory, Russia.

*Kayak and SUP on Windermere near Waterhead.*

# Interactions with other pastimes

Having managed various public open spaces, including nature reserves, parks, recreation grounds, towpaths and trailways, I've come across a few conflicts. Dog walking, cycling and horse-riding are all fairly quiet forms of recreation but their participants don't always appreciate each other's right to use an area. The key is obviously to try not to spoil others' enjoyment and certainly not to endanger others. The problems arise when a few people behave inconsiderately, antagonistically or even dangerously.

Surfers usually follow a code of etiquette we'll list later, but it's understandable that a surfer would feel frustrated to find a novice Supper right across their path, certainly if it happened with the same paddler more than once. Common sense and experience help, along with possibly giving each other's sport a try.

Kayakers and canoeists tend to get on well with Suppers and often paddle or hang out together, a bit like zebras and giraffes. Try not to look down on them metaphorically, especially if you have a long, easily jolted leash!

## Anglers and SUP fishing

You're very likely to come across anglers, particularly inland. It's best to give their equipment a wide berth, particularly on an inflatable board. I tend to smile and, if they look at me, say 'hello'. They're often friendly, happy to tell you what they've caught and interested in what fish you've seen. If they're grumpy it may mean they haven't caught anything. It's a good time to practise how silently you can work your paddle.

Sometimes there's camaraderie and it may be worth mentioning you've probably caused more disturbance to the cormorants than the fish. Inland fishing enthusiasts often regard these hungry fish-eaters as green-eyed mobsters, though most anglers are interested in and very knowledgeable about wildlife. Sadly, those that use fishing lakes can have mixed views on otters. You're less likely to disturb sea anglers but it's still courteous and wise to avoid their space and hooks.

It's important not to disturb the 'reds', grooves in clean gravel where the salmon and trout ('game fish') lay their eggs in winter. Try not to disturb waterweed in spring and summer where other fish, referred to as 'coarse fish', breed. Fish fry also take shelter in weed and they rely on backwaters and other sheltered areas when the general flow is too fast for them.

Salmon were thought not to feed on

their way up rivers to breed, but have been found to consume insects and other invertebrates. Occasionally, if they're not completely worn out, they swim back downstream covered in scars on which fungi grow. They look a very sorry sight, but a few make it back to salt water, which kills the fungus and they can recover ready for another year.

The fishing season has a break from 15 March to 15 June for coarse fish, but varies for game fish on different rivers, though there is usually a break including November, December and January at least. There is no closed season for sea fishing. You may think you're more likely to gain permission to SUP in the closed season. You won't interrupt people fishing legitimately but it is very important not to disturb breeding fish. One significant factor is that anglers often pay to fish and landowners derive an income from this. Ownership will normally cover halfway across the river from their side, though they may own land or fishing rights on both sides.

Compared to some sports, ours is fairly inexpensive after the initial outlay.

Sea anglers near Barafundle Bay, Pembrokeshire.

On really important rivers for trout, such as the Test and Itchen in Hampshire, anglers may pay well over £100 per month, so it seems reasonable to find other places to SUP. However, it also seems fair to allow responsible paddleboarders their share of access, particularly where fishing is less of a concern. We all care about rivers and many paddlers share the sentiment in the old fishing adage: 'a bad day on a river beats a good day at work'.

*Trees, like this elephantine poplar, make good landmarks.*

Some anglers on accessible rivers will be well tucked into bankside vegetation. If going up and downstream, try to remember where they are so you don't suddenly interfere with their lines. Knowing your trees and spotting landmarks will help. As mentioned, litter-picking could smooth the waters.

It is possible to fish from a paddleboard, though in some ways they're not as well designed for this as canoes. They are, however, easier to transport and standing as you paddle gives a better view into the water. There are wide (often 36–40 inches) stable boards made specifically for fishing, with rod holders and room for a cool box. The latter are handy for sitting on as well as keeping your catch (and refreshments) cool. Travel as light as you can, though you may need a head-torch, and an anchor could be useful. Relevant rod or boat licences may be required. Inflatable boards aren't necessarily a good combination with spear-fishing!

*Catching Supper.*

# Wind-dependent watersports

Some sports such as sailing, windsurfing and kitesurfing require reasonably windy days and their colourful sails add to seaside scenes. Supping is generally a sport for fairly calm days, but there is an overlap on days with sufficient breeze for wind-based sports. Kiters can travel at great speeds and this is part of the exhilaration along with the jumps. There are, however, strings attached, literally, and these could cause serious injury if they came swiftly into contact with a paddleboarder.

Where possible, it's worth paddling away from them, though I've often had to teach SUP beginners in areas where we overlap and it is a concern. Many kiters SUP on calm days so they're usually understanding. Kites are more likely to fall in lighter winds and on one occasion I had to dive off my board out of the way while teaching a lesson. The kitesurfer was very apologetic.

# Motorised craft

Paddleboards have become a very popular accessory for boat owners, enhancing their enjoyment of the water. Generally the only problem boats cause is balancing your way through their bow waves. If you're with the boat, you could rope up and ride the waves. If you're not, try to pass on the right of them on rivers/canals, or if easier/safer keep well to the left side, out of their path, even though the right side is the convention.

Jet skis aren't necessarily the perfect accompaniment to a peaceful paddle, but like other motorised craft they may be a source of help if you get into difficulty, particularly in the hands of the RNLI.

*Kites come with strings attached.*

Derwentwater, Cumbria.

# Travel

Supping is a wonderful way to explore new and varied landscapes and see them from a different angle. There is a huge range of scenery in Britain from the majestic lochs of Scotland to the mild sunny shores of the fascinating fossil-rich Jurassic Coast along Dorset and Devon, featuring the famous arch of Durdle Door and the eerie red sandstone rock stacks of Ladram Bay. Across the picture postcard lakes and valleys of Cumbria to the drier climate of the Norfolk broads, with a network of rivers and canals in between, we're not short of destinations for a watery jaunt. Why not try the meandering River Wye on the English/Welsh border, which has long been a favourite for paddlesport? Some areas, such as Warwickshire, have such a good circuit of waterways they should operate SUP hire schemes using a mobile app, similar to those for bicycles.

Cornwall and North Devon offer scenic surf beaches, as does Wales' stunning Pembrokeshire Coast. You could explore the glorious Gower Peninsula, with one highlight being Rhossili Bay where this book's back cover features a tour led by Stuart Gammon (www.adventurestu.com).

Quiet bays and beaches are plentiful around Ireland, which also has the largest lake in the UK, Lough Neagh. There are many lakes along the Shannon, the British Isles' longest river (narrowly ahead of the

Symonds Yat on the River Wye.

# Europe

If you were born under a wandering star and want to spread your wings further, **France** has some wonderful coastline, lakes, canals and rivers that meander through lush landscapes with charming châteaux. Suppers can explore the spectacular limestone scenery of Les Gorges du Verdon or glide down the pristine water of the Dordogne.

The **Netherlands** is another fine SUP destination and not just for its windmills and tulip fields. There are a multitude of canals and this is a great way to explore Amsterdam's charms. Guided SUP tours can be a fascinating, yet calm, way to explore historic cities, somewhat removed from the road traffic. When it comes to memorable canal paddling among unique architecture then it's

Severn, which is slightly longer than the Thames). It also links to Lough Erne and the lively River Liffey by way of calm canal waterways. Look at www.bluewaysireland. org to find details of hundreds of kilometres of scenic inland Irish waterway trails (Blueways) and activity providers.

Ladram Bay, Devon.

also worth a visit to **Italy**, where Venice stands tall.

In **Slovenia** the capital Ljubljana, with its Old Town, makes for a pretty city paddle but the picturesque alpine lakes play the lead role in this country's most romantic scenes. It's the only country with 'love' in its name! I'm indebted to Trudi Beer who sent me photos of Lake Bohinj near the more well-known Lake Bled, after joining me on a tour in Poole Harbour. Long popular with canoeists, **Scandinavia** also has beautiful lakes and rivers to explore including the dramatic Norwegian fjords, the World Heritage Site of Nærøyfjord being the most famous.

**Portugal** is a blissful place to paddle with the quieter, clear, calm waters of the north and the sandy beaches and dramatic caves, stacks and arches of the Algarve. The Mediterranean has much wonderful coastline to offer the Supper with little tide and often particularly calm mornings. A superb paddleboard destination is **Croatia**, known as the 'Land of a Thousand Islands', many of which are sparsely inhabited. It also has stunning ancient cities on the coast. While staying at an independent hotel in Croatia I paid a

Lake Bohinj, Slovenia.

*Classic placid paddle, Lake Holmsjön, Sweden.*

local firm 50 euros for unlimited kayak use for a week and visited eight islands including historic Korčula. Roll on the spread of SUPs. On a Tui holiday in **Sardinia**, a small local outfit on the beach will let you hire SUPs for 10 Euro per hour without any limits on how far you can go.

For stress-free paddling, a good option is to stay at a hotel that offers SUP. Providers such as Neilson, which specialise in activity holidays, will have kit available to use free of charge. Obviously they will impose limits on how far you can go, partly for your own safety as well as keeping their equipment secure. We stayed in Syvota on mainland **Greece** and were able to SUP any day in a large bay and go on organised tours around an island. Other sports holiday specialists, such as Mark Warner, are available and some smaller companies offer SUP holidays and tours.

THE PADDLEBOARD BIBLE

*Lake Lucerne — when it comes to scenic lakes, Switzerland is no slouch.*

Paddling the Havasu Creek near the Colorado River in the Grand Canyon, Arizona.

# The wider world

Beyond Europe there is an endless number of destinations to unleash or leash your itchy feet, if your budget allows. Every continent offers opportunities from visiting world famous wonders to finding authentic experiences that are special to their region. With this new mode of travel you can witness traditional ways of life without causing disturbance. It's prudent to check the latest travel advice for some areas.

Moving further around the Med, if you like your

Supping served with a fascinating helping of cultural interest, there are no shortage of places around the Middle Eastern shores or along the coast of North Africa. Off the tourist trail there's the lure of

Lanzarote's volcanic rocks.

**Lebanon** with some good sheltered water and surf locations. **Morocco** has accommodation to suit all budgets and waves for every ability, particularly on its Atlantic coast. Another fairly short flight destination with great weather is the **Canaries**. Look out for knobbly volcanic rocks on down-winders in Lanzarote.

Deeper into Africa, the intrepid may be tempted by a white water trip down the Nile in **Uganda** or to visit its main source from Lake Victoria. Paddleboarding is well established in **South Africa** on the inland waters and surf beaches of Cape Town and the significantly warmer waters off Durban. Off Africa's east coast many hotels and local providers in **Mauritius** offer paddleboards and this is a wonderful way to investigate its mangroves, turquoise lagoons and tropical rivers.

Asia has played its part in the rise of SUP, not merely because many boards are made there. The quantity and quality of SUP provision has seen a marked increase in recent years. The beautiful lagoons of **Bali** and the islands of southern **Thailand**, with their incredible rock formations, are popular spots. Away from the more visited areas, there are many hidden SUP delights. In **India** you could try an organised river tour past ancient temples and through dense forest, before reaching the Bay of Bengal. SUP has become very popular in **China**, which hosted the ISA World SUP and Paddleboard Championship in 2018.

Moving across to North America, there are wonderful lakes and rivers to paddle on right across **Canada**, but the west side has some of the world's most scenic.

Early mornings are a SUP photographer's heaven when mirror calm conditions can prevail. North America also has the Great Lakes. These can become challengingly windswept and waveswept enough to surf. Hence Chicago, at the base of Lake Michigan, is known as the 'Windy City'. California has some sumptuous landscapes to explore and beaches to go surfin' in the **USA**, including Santa Barbara, Malibu and San Diego. This state also has Lake Tahoe, where the crystal clear water reflecting rugged scenery makes this one of the most photographed SUP locations on the planet. You could also trace Supping back to its (generally accepted!) roots, by heading to Hawaii.

The clear warm waters and soft sandy beaches of the Caribbean make it a wonderful destination. Several hotels in **Antigua** offer access to paddleboards for all guests, if you're looking to hone your skills on a relaxing holiday or persuade your partner to take up Supping in between sipping cocktails! Alternatively you could sample the rich marine ecosystems of the **Turks and Caicos Islands** or the neighbouring **Bahamas** with a SUP and a snorkel. See if you can spot an Atlantic spotted dolphin, one of several species that may be sighted here. From December to March the weather is reliably good, with September being the peak of the hurricane season.

The small tropical town of Sayulita is regarded as the SUP Mecca of **Mexico**. This is quite an honour in a country with 14,500km of coastline, including excellent surf beaches and azure waters. Central America has many excellent places to

8 • SENSE OF ADVENTURE!

paddleboard to suit a range of budgets.

Supping is a great way to view **Brazil's** famously striking locations. You could paddle in the shadow of Sugarloaf Mountain or pass by Ipanema Beach in Rio de Janeiro. Over on the west, **Colombia** also has remarkable biodiversity to entice a SUP adventurer, with guided tours in the Santa Marta region. You can listen for howler monkeys and many exotic birds on the Rio Buritaca or explore other rivers flowing down from the Sierra Nevada de Santa Marta, passing through areas of jungle that have changed little in hundreds of years. Seasoned watersport holiday organiser, Andy Gratwick, describes **Peru** as having one

*Explore the Colombian jungle with Paddle Boarding Santa Marta.*

of the most wave-rich coastlines on the planet. SUP surfers can test their skills on mellow beach breaks or barrelling waves moving from left to right as you look from the shore. Peru has twice hosted the ISA World Championship.

Heading across to the South West Pacific, there are wonderful destinations to replace our winter blues with warm

*The girl from Ipanema SUPs by.*

azure waters. **Tahiti** is a paddleboarder's paradise, with much of the shoreline a beautiful lagoon sheltered by an offshore reef, with the exception of a few great surf spots. **Fiji** is also acclaimed as a Supper's dream come true with flat water, down-winders and surf.

For its variety of stunning scenery, including fjords, glaciers, geysers and volcanoes, **New Zealand** is, of course, well worth a visit. The subtropical climate of New Zealand's northern reaches warms the waters of the Bay of Islands with its sheltered coves and inlets. On the north coast of the country's South Island, you could explore the stunning coastline of Abel Tasman National Park. With beautiful bays and beaches, it has long been popular with kayakers and walkers, for trips of one day or several, with Department of Conservation huts to stay in along the way with other travellers.

I was lucky in that back in the early '90s, you could buy a 'hut pass' and set off. It has now become so popular that you have to book well in advance. Supping

*Lake Wanaka on New Zealand's South Island is a stunning place for a SUP.*

*Fur seals add to the splendour of the Abel Tasman coastline.*

would be a blissful way to enjoy its clear sheltered waters.

Much of my travelling, including eight months 'Down Under', was done before Supping became established in **Australia**, though surfing was very much a part of Australian culture. Both sides of this vast country have extensive inland waters to explore. Tasmania would be a terrific place to take SUP stuff. The capital, Hobart, has a very attractive shoreline, long popular with the sailing fraternity. 'Tassie', as Aussies refer to it, also has one of the most beautiful coastal views I have ever seen, Wineglass Bay in Freycinet National Park. At that time accommodation there was very limited. Now the park has a lodge with cabins, along with other nearby options, and SUP tours and rental will enable you to admire

the amazing life in this Marine Park.

Finding beautiful places to paddle may leave you monetarily poorer, but much richer in marvellous memories.

## Taking your board abroad

One way to travel is to take your SUP equipment with you. This can give you the freedom to plan all-manner of once-in-a-lifetime SUP experiences and possibly see some of the wildlife mentioned in a previous chapter. Inflatables are much easier to carry. If you become a paddleboard instructor, you may want to find your dream location in the world to spread the word of SUP, or take your CV.

Some inflatable boards roll or fold up

very compactly and come in good bags. It's recommended to have the valve in the down/open setting when flying. A three-piece paddle can be relatively easy to pack. Make sure the blade doesn't dig into a rolled up board. A pump may fit in with clothing or roll within an inflatable, which might not exceed your luggage weight limit, though do check. If there's room, towels and clothes can wrap around your board in its bag. Some people wrap the whole bag in cellophane stretch wrap. Special lined travel bags are another option.

## Top travel tips

● Make sure you have paperwork to show any extra luggage is paid for. It can be a bad start to the holiday if you have a difficult discussion at check-in while a queue of your frustrated fellow fliers builds up behind you. Contact the airline if you have particular concerns.
● If travelling as a group, be very careful about sharing luggage allowance.
● Bag, double bag, line the bag, wrap and label everything carefully. The busy baggage handlers may not treat it as they would their own. It may still get ripped open, but it will strengthen your case with insurers if you've taken reasonable precautions, but there is still damage.
● Check your insurance, as sports equipment may not be covered. Contact them if unsure.

As SUP's popularity grows, there are more opportunities to hire equipment. Doing some research, checking websites and contacting hotels may help.

*SUP from Wineglass Bay in Tasmania's Freycinet.*

# 9 LIVE TO SUP ANOTHER DAY

Supping is a relatively safe mode of transport and sport. Before it took off, I went on a three-day kitesurfing course. Shortly afterwards, someone my partner knew ended up in a coma from kiting (which has become somewhat safer now). I felt that she would rather I grew tomatoes after that. Paddleboarding seemed like a good compromise. It isn't entirely without risks, but with thought, preparation and care, it can be as stress-free or exciting as you want it to be.

If you're embarking on a SUP trip, particularly alone, it's very wise to let someone know your plans, including your route and when you should be back. Keep them informed if your plans change and when you're back. There's a Royal Yachting Association (RYA) app called Safetrx, recommended by HM Coastguard, in which you can specify you're a paddleboarder and give a brief description of what you look like. You can then input your route, with waypoints on a map and your emergency contact details. Your contact will receive text updates and the Coastguard will have access to the information. It is free to download and use. You may also wish to take a Personal Locator Beacon which, when activated, sends an alert via satellite to the Coastguard.

# Site or route assessment

When planning or setting out on a paddle it's important to assess the area you'll be paddling in. This could be broken down into the acronym LETS:

- **Location** – type, topography, hazards, access, entry/exit points
- **Elements or Environment** – weather/forecast, wind, tides/flow/currents, air/water temperature, water quality
- **Third party** – bathers, anglers, boats, other watersports, wildlife, livestock
- **Surface** – water surface (calm, choppy, wavy), shoreline, river/sea bed (muddy, pebbly, etc), depth, rocks, structures, vegetation

These factors will vary in likely significance from place to place. Other considerations include:

- People paddling in your group – ability and experience (particularly of the type of location), health/fitness and equipment/clothing.
- Available time and daylight.

Beware the jagged rock, my son! The jaws that bite, the claws that catch!

# Hazards and health risks

Piers can be fun to steer under, but structures may be unsafe and often require care.

Here are some of the potential problems:

- **Hazards** – fog, strong offshore winds, large waves, rapids, weirs, lightning, masonry, rocks, structures, thorns, people participating in other pastimes, obstacles in rivers or livestock along them, litter.
- **Health risks** – sunburn, cuts, sprains, jellyfish, weever fish, sunstroke, pollution, Weil's disease, Lyme's disease, discarded hypodermic needles, hepatitis B, hypothermia, cold water shock, drowning.

Some could be thought of as both, such as sharks and crocodiles!

Thorns from hawthorn or blackthorn (sloe bush) may be a hazard to you, but could be more of a problem to your inflatable board. They're more likely to leave a slow puncture when they come out, but a faster puncture could leave you with a big problem if you can't make it to safety or get help easily. Thankfully this would be extremely unlikely as ISUPs are tough. With a companion, depending on the size of their board, you could tow a flaccid board or position it across the other board if there is room for both of you and it. Eventually you might need to deflate and roll it up. Alone with a deflated board and a long swim, you may be able to attach it to a buoy. Bear in mind, of course, that your life is more important than the board.

Proceed with care if cattle are in a river, particularly bulls or cows with young. Bullocks tend to get out of the

*Always look out for danger!*

way of a paddle group but can be bolder, friendly or curious if you're alone. If you have a dog it may be seen as a threat; they also sometimes see children in this way, being similarly smaller. Keep calm and head or walk around them if you can. Consider heading back or, on a down-streamer, sit and wait for them to move on. We rely on farmers for access, so only use your paddle to defend yourself as a last resort if charged aggressively.

Find out if there are weirs, drops or millraces on river routes, particularly when the general flow is strong and their grasp may be harder to escape. Plan, look and also listen for weirs. Remember 'There's an old mill by the stream...' If you see a tall old building it may be worth assessing the situation on foot.

Where trees have fallen in the water be particularly careful. There may only be a branch near the surface or protruding but you could become snagged or entangled. When water can pass through an obstacle like a tree but you can't, walk around. These features are known as 'strainers' (like a food strainer, the water passes through but the pasta or vegetables are retained). If you come off your board in flowing water, a log near the surface can pin you under with fatal consequences.

Here are more details of some health risks of varying degrees of severity:

● **Jellyfish** tentacles can sting, though those of the common large white/ transparent barrel jellyfish don't usually affect humans. The compass jellyfish, also shown, has a sting generally a bit worse than nettles. Rinse the area with seawater, then soak for 30 minutes in very warm water. Be careful if you see a creature with a blue tinge, as there is a small chance it could be a Portuguese man-o'-war, which resembles jellyfish, is shaped like a bulbous pasty and has a powerful sting.

● **Weever fish** are fairly docile, peaceably living in the sea among sand or mud. However, they have venomous spines, which they inject into your foot if you have the misfortune to step on one. Your entire leg may feel numb and the pain can last for a few days, but they rarely become infected. Rinse with sea water

*Barrel jellyfish and compass jellyfish.*

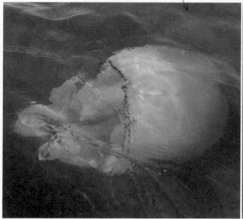
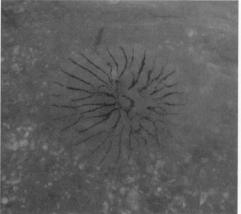

(not fresh). Remove spines with tweezers or the edge of a plastic card, then soak in hot water for 30 minutes. You could take paracetamol or ibuprofen if these are OK for you.

● **Weil's disease** is a bacterial infection that may be caught from water contaminated by the urine of infected animals, particularly rats. On urban watercourses protect your feet, cover skin breaks with waterproof plasters and try to keep water out of your mouth and eyes. Hand sanitiser may be worth using before eating. Symptoms can resemble flu, including headache, chills and muscle pain. It is important to tell medical staff you may have been exposed to Weil's. Most cases are mild but a small few become very serious. I know someone who works on rivers who became badly affected, with liver and kidney damage. Fortunately he was young and fit and made a full recovery.

● **Tick bites**, which leave a round red mark around the bite, may cause Lyme's disease. Remove the tick as soon as possible with tweezers or a small plastic removal tool, available from pharmacies and vets and worth adding to the first

aid kit on your dry-bag list. Covering skin and using insect repellents with DEET are worth considering in areas such as saltmarsh, long grass or scrub which deer frequent. If you become unwell let medics know it may be from a tick.

● **Algae** occur naturally in water, but where you get a thick, unpleasant bloom of blue-green algae, this can produce toxins. Try to avoid swallowing and contact with your skin, particularly your face. Rinse skin as soon as possible and clean your hands thoroughly before eating. Seek medical advice if you feel unwell, such as irritation of the skin, blistered lips or mouth ulcers, vomiting or diarrhoea.

● **Cold water shock** is a danger if someone is suddenly immersed in cold waters, in Britain for instance. Most of us would gasp, but in more extreme cases people can lose control of their breathing and gasp repeatedly and rapidly. If you take a gulp of water into your lungs you may drown. Wearing suitable clothing and particularly a buoyancy aid will reduce the risk. If you are aware that you may have cold water shock, lie on your back and only move gently, sculling with your arms to steer, until your breathing normalises.

More prolonged exposure to cold water or conditions can cause **hypothermia,** which occurs when the body's core temperature falls below 35°C. Initial symptoms include shivering and pale, cold skin, followed by stiffness, disorientation and unconsciousness. If someone is shivering uncontrollably, get them warm by sharing body heat, helping them into dry clothing, covering their head and using a survival bag or foil blanket if you have one.

# Reducing risks

Carrying out a 'Risk Assessment' may sound a bit too work-related to apply in your spare time, but could help you 'Carry on Supping'.

Even done informally, it is a great way to at least consider potential risks, how likely they are and how serious, and, very usefully, how to reduce and manage them. This is the methodology:

- **First, think of all notable risks** on a paddle, many of which will vary with the venue and conditions, and list them in a table.
- **Assign a score** to how likely each is on a scale of 1 (very unlikely), 2 (unlikely), 3 (not unlikely) to 4 (quite probable).
- **Score them for severity,** from 1 (minor), 2 (quite serious), 3 (very serious) to 4 (life changing or fatal). This will vary with some risks such as a head injury.
- **Multiply the likelihood** and severity scores for each risk. (This just highlights the element of risk as for the point below.)
- **For all risks,** think of and action ways to reduce them (prevention and cure), particularly those with the highest scores.

Here is a table with some examples:

| Risk | Likelihood x severity | Control measures |
|---|---|---|
| Sunburn | 3 × 1 = 3 | Sunscreen and/or clothing |
| Cut foot | 2 × 2 = 4 | Neoprene boots, first aid kit, avoid rocks, take care near structures |
| Hypo-thermia | 2 × 3 = 6 | Check forecast, clothing, foil blanket, share warmth, take food |
| Drowning | 1 × 4 = 4 | Buoyancy aid, appropriate leash, experience, swimming ability, first aid training |
| Head injury | 1 × 3 = 3 | Avoid hazards, venue choice, helmet, take bandages/dressings |
| Weil's disease | 1 × 3 = 3 | Dress cuts, avoid swallowing and facial contact with water in urban areas, carry a card and make sure medical staff are aware of the possibility |
| Pulled muscle | 2 × 2 = 4 | Warm-up exercises, then stretching before paddle |

As well as risk assessments, companies providing tours should have an Emergency Action Plan.

# Accidents

**It is well worth attending first aid and safety courses,** then the need or desire to help can be backed up with knowledge and understanding of the best way to go about it.

A casualty may be someone you know or someone you're responsible for. You'll want to do all you can. However, the first thing to consider is your own safety. You could make the situation worse if you quickly become an additional casualty.

One recommended way to remember what to do in the correct order is DR'S ABCD.

**D: DANGER.** As mentioned, assess for dangers and make the situation safer if possible.

**R: RESPONSE.** Find out how responsive the casualty is:

- Are they are alert?
- Do they respond to your voice – 'Hello, can you hear me?'
- If not, see whether they respond to pain – a pat on the forearm or shoulder, or a tap of your foot on theirs, should establish this without causing injury or offence, if not try a small pinch on the earlobe

If they are responsive, the rescue or towing procedures described in the 'Advanced Techniques' chapter may be needed.

**S:** if they are unresponsive **SHOUT** for help. You're then into first aid territory, for which attending a course is by far the best advice, but below is a brief summary of current guidelines:

**A:** open their **AIRWAY** by extending their chin while holding their head back. (Clear anything from their mouth.)

**B:** listen for **BREATHING**.

*Do they need saving or are they drowsing?*

If yes, place the casualty in the 'recovery position'. Make sure their head is down and tilted to one side. This is particularly important if they are wet and may need to cough out water. Keep them warm to avoid hypothermia. You may have a hat, towel or foil blanket in your dry-bag. Make sure they get medical help (*see secondary drowning on page 197*).

The recovery position is a safe way to place a casualty, particularly if they are unconscious:

1 **Place the arm nearest to you** so that the elbow is bent and the palm faces upward (compromise if the arm is not very flexible).

2 **Place their other hand** against their cheek, supported by your hand.

3 **Lift their furthest knee,** then bring this towards you to roll them onto their side, while protecting their face (see photos).

4 **Tilt their head back** to open their airway and continue to monitor their breathing and pulse. Remember to keep them warm.

If not they are not breathing, call 999 for an ambulance if onshore or the Coastguard if offshore. Alternatively ask someone nearby to do this and to come back to confirm it. State that you have an unconscious/not breathing casualty and your location. (In many countries, including most in Europe, phoning 112 will connect to the emergency services or be forwarded to them, for instance to 911 in North America or 000 in Australia. 111 can be called for a situation that isn't an emergency.) Raise your arms like a letter 'Y' to a rescue helicopter if you need help.

*The 'recovery position', as described.*

If you have received first aid training and know how to, you could perform a combination of chest compressions and rescue breaths.

**C: CIRCULATION.** Breathing is a higher priority, but after this problems such as bleeding can be dealt with.

**D: DEFIBRILLATOR.** If you have a casualty who isn't breathing and a defibrillator is available, you will probably need to phone 999 to get the code for it. Once open, switch it on and it will give audible instructions. Although you don't need training to follow these, it is clearly better to have had it. Depending on the situation and availability this would be a higher priority than dealing with wounds.

# Casualty in water

The situation can be more difficult if the casualty is still in the water. Life saving courses are very useful and it can be enjoyable to practise with a club. I trained with a club affiliated to the Royal Life Saving Society, but there are other bodies, such as the Surf Life Saving Association of Great Britain.

If you encounter a casualty in water, you could use the rescue technique, described in 'Advanced Techniques' (*see page 44*), to bring them onto your board. Consider how near the shore and possible help you are. You'll have to assess what's best in your situation and think of your own health and safety. Hopefully you'll never be in these situations but the more idea of what to do, the better chance the casualty will stand. You can only do your best in what are difficult, traumatic circumstances.

People should always be checked

## RNLI RESCUES

According to RNLI statistics, between 2011 and 2015 there were no fatalities involving paddleboarding. There were, however, 50 incidents with 31 lifeboat launches in the UK and one in the Republic of Ireland, which they also cover. As the sport grows, there is a likelihood that these figures may increase, so take care. Reassuringly, few people drown while wearing buoyancy aids or doing organised activities. Generally the number of drowning victims is reducing, probably due to awareness, training and help provision.

medically after water inhalation.
Secondary drowning (up to 72 hours later),
when water has entered the lungs, can
be a risk.

The Tarcoles River, Costa Rica,
viewed from 'Crocodile Bridge'.

## CHECKLIST

To summarise some of the most
important safety measures you
can take:

- [ ] Check weather and tides
- [ ] Choose and assess your location
  carefully
- [ ] Tell someone your plans
- [ ] Take a mobile phone in a waterproof
  wallet
- [ ] Know how to call for help – 999 (UK)
  or 112
- [ ] Wear/take appropriate clothing
- [ ] Wear a leash and buoyancy aid

Paddling with others will greatly reduce
risks. Attempting challenging paddles
with less than three people makes
problems harder to deal with.

# Insurance

It's a good idea to have insurance that
includes third party cover. If it covers
other countries this could also be
useful to you.

Membership of British Canoeing
includes insurance detailed on the BC
website. The British Stand Up Paddleboarding Association (BSUPA) provides
insurance (worldwide excluding North
America) to individual members along
with other benefits (newsletter, organising
training and events, holiday discounts)
as well as helping to develop the sport.
There are other options including special
packages from commercial insurers. If
you start a paddling group it's even more
important to be covered.

If you have travel insurance, check
what it provides. Crocodile damage to
you or your board might not be covered!

If there are three or more it's easier
to treat a casualty and get help.

# 10 THRILLS, SKILLS AND SPILLS!

Australians have an inspiring campaign called 'Life. Be in it.', encouraging people to live healthier and more active lifestyles.

If you want to live that life in the fast lane, with more of a rush from your paddleboard and your adrenal glands there are several ways to experience this: SUP surf, white water and races. You may also have seen or heard of 'foils', which were mentioned in the equipment chapter (*see page 55*).

# SUP surfing

One of the wonderful facets of paddleboarding is the variety of activities it encompasses. The sport sprang up from surfing and this is one of the most exhilarating ways to enjoy balancing on a board. It's also terrific for developing your skills, balance and fitness.

If you have surfed or taken surf training this will be very helpful, but as a Supper you will at least be used to balancing on and steering a board. Supping is attracting a new wave of people to the thrill of surfing!

A useful exercise is to practise paddling in the surf stance, initially on flat water then gradually progress to small waves. Whereas in normal Supping your feet are either side of the handle, for surfing one goes behind the other. Place one foot across the board just in front of the handle pointing about 45° forward and the other a step back two or three feet (60–90cm) pointing across the board. If you find this difficult, try a compromise between SUP and surf stances at first.

Surfing is dynamic and you need to be able to shuffle your feet around somewhat, forward and backward, taking the weight off your feet evenly,

Life in the fast lane.

you're ready to look for a beach with a few waves. As indicated in the chapter on waves, some of the best beaches for surfing occur on the western side of landmasses. As a novice SUP surfer you want fairly small waves on safe beaches. Rocky shores can send up some inviting waves, but you want a painless landing and to finish with your equipment in good order.

Avoid busy surf beaches, where you may get in the way of experienced surfers, but watching them can be informative, as well as strangely relaxing. Most surf beaches have quiet times of the day, week or year. If you can reach a suitable beach on a weekday morning outside of school holidays, you'll probably find some space. The chapter on wind and waves will help you understand where and when the waves will suit you, as will webcams. The best waves are described as spilling.

so become used to doing this. Have your front knee bent for stability.

Also try leaning forward and backward while paddling. Try assuming the stance both ways: left in front and right in front. It will be an advantage if you can manage both ways but you will probably find one comes more naturally. It's probably best to have the leash on the back foot in your most assured stance.

Once you're comfortable paddling in surf stance and moving your feet,

Of course you could book a lesson or you may prefer to go with friends, particularly if they are more experienced

SUP surfing will develop your balance!

THE PADDLEBOARD BIBLE

Newgale Beach, Pembrokeshire is renowned for surfing, but is often quiet on weekday mornings.

and can give tips. At first you should be looking for waves that are only 30–60cm high. If the waves are coming in parallel to the shore that will make life easier too. Having identified novice-friendly waves, making your way out through them is the next challenge.

Use a lull in them to walk your board out to the side of the main waves. To do this, point the board into the waves at around 75° from the shore (much less and you'll be turned back to shore, but at right angles the board could come up at you). Hold your paddle on top of the board, paddle handle to the front. Avoid the board handle, as this could strain your wrist. Press the back of the board down as each wave comes to meet you. When the water comes up to your lower thigh, mount your board, then stay on your knees or stand and purposefully paddle through the waves at right angles. You may eventually want to progress to diving under waves, termed duck-diving, on a rigid board.

Surfers have no shortage of phrases and words that might not make sense to others. If you prefer to surf with your right foot forward this is known as 'goofy-footed'.

If you are more comfortable with the right foot back, known as 'regular', paddle out to the right side of your chosen waves; if left, paddle out to the left of them. Then (drum roll) brace yourself for some exhilarating wave action:

**1** **Stand in the normal SUP stance** and watch the waves.

**2** **Identify where the waves** are building to the right height and position yourself slightly further out on your chosen side.

**3** **Pick your wave** when it is a little way off, not one that will pass you too soon.

**4** **Angle yourself at 45°** toward the shore and toward where you're hoping to catch the wave.

**5** **Paddling on the same side** as your normal back foot, try to build up speed so you will be travelling at a similar speed to the wave as it catches up with you.

**6** **Before it catches up** with you change to your surf stance.

**7** **You should naturally veer** so that as the wave comes you are roughly facing the shore, with no need for bow strokes unless you overdo veering.

**8** **Lean on your front foot** and feel the whoosh as you ride your wave!

**9** **If it overtakes you,** try to stay balanced as the one behind might give you an even better ride, possibly taking you to the shore.

**10** **By leaning forward** you can go faster, leaning back will slow you down.

*Start at 45° and build up speed.*

*Squat to help with balance as the wave comes.*

As you approach the shore, you may want to kneel down and either step off before you reach it or turn around and go again. You don't want to jolt off as your board hits the shore, especially on a busy beach. This may cause injury or damage as well as embarrassment. With practice you can remain standing and either pick the right moment to step off and grab your board smoothly or turn around and head out again, returning to the SUP stance. We'll come to surf etiquette, but paddle out giving others surfing in a wide berth.

One advantage of the surf stance is it allows you to pivot your hips and turn the board. Stepping toward the back of your board will make this more effective. Leaning slightly into the turn will add to this effect, such as when bike riding or skiing. Having a paddle also helps with turning and speed, but you can also use it to brace against the water by squatting lower and holding the edge of the blade front side down against the surface. This extra point of contact will help you

to balance or you can hold it above the water ready to brace when needed. You may want your paddle a little shorter than for touring (perhaps 5cm) as you'll be squatting more.

You can also try riding in more diagonally to the shore, if the wind doesn't take you that way anyway. Eventually you may aspire to practise turning both at the bottom and near the top of the front face of waves using wide strokes, bow strokes and your hips as well as bracing your paddle.

As well as specific surf sessions, you can have a quick go at the end of coastal tours when it doesn't matter if you get wet. Generally in our cool waters you'll require a wetsuit for surfing which will

*Brace your paddle as an extra point of contact.*

protect you from scrapes as well as the cold. From a safe distance, bow waves from passing boats can now be a source of fun, as you switch to the surf stance, rather than a destabilising interference. Downwind paddles may now be interspersed with exhilarating wave-riding.

Don't be too ambitious too soon. Surfing will develop your lung capacity, but if you crash under a large wave while already out of breath, you could drown. Surfing may be considered a cool sport, but you have to stay safe to enjoy it. You may want to consider wearing a helmet, available from watersports retailers such as kayak shops. This is particularly advisable if there are rocks. As a beginner, don't surf alone and ideally use beaches with lifeguards present to practise your skills in relative safety.

Events to look out for are the Porthcawl SUP Surf Classic, in South Wales, and the more established Irish SUP Surf Classic at Enniscrone, County Sligo, near the Moy Estuary. Just up river, the bridge at Ballina is a great place to watch otters demonstrate their skills.

*Experienced surfer riding along the front of a wave.*

# Surfing etiquette

**To rule the waves, don't waive the rules!** There is an established etiquette to surfing. Following this helps avoid injury to yourself and others. It will help you avoid unpleasant conflicts too, particularly with locals to the beach you're on. As a Supper, and particularly a novice SUP surfer, try to avoid getting in the way of experienced surfers.

Take your turn in the line-up.

1 **Choose an appropriate place** for your skill level.

2 **'Priority boarding'** – who has priority or first shot at a wave? Normally the person closest to the peak of the wave, which will tend to be the one furthest out. If a surfer without a paddle is already standing, they have priority. If you're intending to head diagonally right, have a glance to your left to check whether someone is already surfing.

3 **Take turns** – you will sometimes see surfers waiting in line like a queue. If you mess up your turn you have to go to the back of the queue.

4 **Don't snake** – this is where someone curves around another to get into the priority position. Like queue jumping it is particularly annoying as the 'snake' will probably have a reasonable skill level and should know better.

5 **Don't be a wave hog** – as a Supper you are well equipped to take more than your share of waves. Don't.

6 **Communicate** – chatting to others creates a friendly atmosphere and can help avoid misunderstandings. Surfers tend to be sociable.

7 **Respect the locals** – it's unwise to annoy them. They may also be a good source of advice. Be considerate to other beach users.

8 **Try to hold on to your board** – always wear a leash, though not the coiled ones as these can get caught around you.

9 **Apologise** – if you unintentionally affect someone's ride and can't steer out of their way in time, be quick to say or gesture an apology.

10 **Respect the area** – drive and park with care. Don't litter.

# Carrying your board

SUP surfing may involve carrying your board across an exposed beach. Many people prefer to have the board on their downwind side, though on the upwind side you can brace it against your hip and use your paddle to help control the front end. On a long carry it's good to swap occasionally. If there are two of you, carrying two boards with one of you holding the fronts of the boards and one the backs is a good option.

*The constant need to think ahead replaces everyday stresses with adrenaline.*

# White water

In North America Supping white water is one of the fastest growing branches of the sport, so it is worth considering. As with surfing, it can be totally absorbing as you need complete focus. Like fell running downhill, it demands continual quick thinking and forward planning. Water that is slightly white can:

*To boldly go between boulders.*

- be a fun and thrilling challenge.
- develop your balance, fitness, SUP skills and strokes.
- sharpen your reflexes.
- improve your feel for river hydrology.
- involve Supping in more dramatic, beautiful places.

There may be small swift sections on otherwise calm rivers where a little understanding and experience of white water can be extremely useful. You may have an opportunity to test your balance where the flow across the river alternates between fast downstream currents and slower upstream eddies. You may also find accessible places on fast rivers where there is a manageable stretch between the mayhem. The previously mentioned UK Rivers Guidebook website is a good source of information.

White water is more associated with canoes and kayaks. If you have such experience it will be a big advantage. You may also know suitable places or could use a seated craft to check out possibilities for white water SUP, including depth and difficulty, though these will vary with flow. Low water levels could be too shallow and high water could be a hell of a challenge! From a standing position you can at least see hazards better and your legs won't be trapped, which is one cause of serious problems for kayakers in these conditions. It's good to be able to assess the route from the bank too.

For white water there is a grading system from 1 to 6, where 1 is flat water. As a Supper, you are pretty limited to Grade 2 unless you're experienced and accomplished. Grade 2 will have some currents too strong for upstream paddling but won't tend to have obstacles or drops, unlike Grade 3. Anything higher than 3 could be considered extreme, though there are photos of Suppers shooting over large drops.

Safety is, of course, a huge consideration. **Beware hazards such as mills, weirs and snags in trees.** Think about the availability of medical help and take appropriate measures to reduce risks, including safety equipment and a first aid kit.

Other than when playing in safe, fairly tame conditions, a watersport specific helmet that includes forehead coverage is more than advisable. Make sure it

*Waist belt released with a toggle.*

fits securely and comfortably. Rocky rivers are not for the faint-hearted or bare-footed. Wear strong protective footwear, such as good neoprene boots. You will also need an easily released or self-releasing (when under high tension) leash that can be attached to a waist belt or preferably a velcro chest strap. This should be separate to your buoyancy aid. Don't wear an ankle leash. If one wrapped around a branch or other obstacle and you came off your board in a strong flow, you might be unable to free the leash, increasing the risks of serious injury (or worse) considerably.

A good buoyancy aid (personal flotation device) is also a must (arm bands don't suffice!). A winter wetsuit will help cushion any blows and protect you from the cold. Knee and elbow pads are a good idea.

At least one person in the group should be very competent in white water, preferably more, especially if there are several of you. Never attempt white water alone and take a throw bag to help others. Practise throwing them. It will waste valuable time if they fall short or downstream of the person needing them, or if they become snagged in rocks or trees. Ropes need to be thick, strong and buoyant. Over many years, seated paddlers have developed all manner of rescue skills using ropes. It's worth taking a knife, in case you become entangled. A whistle can be used to call for help with six blasts given at minute intervals. The reply is three blasts but don't stop until it arrives. Repeat the six if no response. A paddle can be used to help rescue someone just out of arm's reach and adjustable ones could be quickly extended if necessary. Safety training is extremely advisable and there are courses specific to white water SUP.

Given that white water can be very cold and falling in is very possible, you may want to wear a drysuit. Once inside, hold the neck open and squat to force out air, so your legs aren't more buoyant than the rest of you. Some paddlers wear strong neoprene boots over the boots that are

part of the suit. This gives your feet more much needed protection, but also helps prevent leaks in the suit's feet which would defeat its purpose and can be expensive to have properly repaired. Try to avoid thorn bushes and brambles.

You'll need a fairly robust board. It must be controllable so you will want at least one fin, but a long fragile fin wouldn't be very good. Three plastic fins, no longer/deeper than 10cm, ideally less for the lateral fins, are a good option. Swept back flexible fins lack the control of hard fins, but are less likely to catch on rocks. Retractable fins can break with a diagonal impact. There are boards specifically designed for white water, either rigid or inflatable, short and wide for manoeuvrability and stability, with high rails (sides). These tend to have an even number of fins. As you're rarely moving in a straight line a central fin is less needed.

Rigid boards can have more specialised shapes, though they are harder to carry which can be a factor in

The tripod stance – try to maintain a wide triangle, even when swapping sides.

THE PADDLEBOARD BIBLE

## CAUTION!

As a beginner, find a swift section, possibly beyond a bridge, where the flow becomes steady before long. Weirs should be avoided. As well as strong currents, there may be metalwork or other hazards by them.

**STEER CLEAR OF A WEIR!**

*Going down on one knee.*

switching sides to form a tripod on the other side. If you bring your paddle back too far, you'll form more of a straight line with your feet which is a recipe for a wobble. As with surfing, you may want your paddle slightly shorter than for touring as you'll be squatting more.

Where a river speeds up between narrowing sides, bridge arches or obstacles, the safest place to aim downstream tends to be the middle of the V-shape that forms on the surface between them. To the sides of the flows there will be eddies. These are advantageous if you want to head up river because they flow that way as the water circulates back from the flow. Eddies can also be useful places to enter and exit the river, or when you wish to break out from the fast flow. However, this can be tricky.

the terrain that goes with white water. The other advantage of inflatables is that they tend not to suffer damage on rocks. However, they can become somewhat stuck against a rock, unlike a smooth plastic-coated board.

Stability is crucial. It helps to have your feet positioned in a wide diagonal stance. Use your paddle to form a triangle with them like a tripod. You'll move your feet more than when touring, for instance

*Aim for the centre of a downstream V-shape.*

Crossing the eddy line means transferring your weight at the right moment. Squatting lower will help you balance as usual. Angling your paddle to guide your board can be more effective than driving strokes and makes it easier to maintain the tripod. In places it is possible to point your board into the flow and move across the river by adjusting the angle of your blade in relation to the flow. This is known as a 'ferry glide'.

Avoid doing this too close below a fall without a downstream 'V'. In these areas, circulating water could pull and

## TIP TIP!
..........................

It's always best to put slightly more of your weight on the down-stream side when crossing the flow. This may seem strange, but if you lean into the flow it will press on the rail on your upstream side and can quickly tip you over. In eddies the flow is back upstream so you should apply more weight upstream (away from the flow).

hold you down if you come off. Another danger is getting your foot trapped. Try not to walk in deep water and bear in mind the depth may increase suddenly as you approach a fast section.

If you come off your board and your leash releases and you can't get back to your board, lie on your back with your head lifted only slightly, just enough to see ahead, and your feet raised together pointing downstream. Use your arms to steer and avoid fallen

*Anthony Ing remaining balanced on a not so small fall. Even Supping wee drops it's easy to topple over!*

trees. Use your feet to push off boulders. If the water becomes deep and obstacle free you could swim on your front. Try to retain your paddle. There's more chance your board will lodge somewhere it can be recovered from. At the first safe opportunity, head to a side where you can climb ashore. Remaining calm but determined will help. If remounting your board, turn onto your front, but don't put your feet down.

> **Don't risk your limbs or life to recover equipment.**

I had a training session with Anthony Ing who runs Stand Up Paddle Board UK. Britain's leading white water SUP instructor, Anthony recommends trying features on your knees, then progress to one foot and one knee, then standing, but squat very low as you come out of a drop to avoid falling backward. Think about what you could do better and try again. Mastering a feature can bring a satisfying sense of achievement. Going from one feature to another, you may want to drop back down to one knee or kneeling.

Training is extremely advisable. Good places to experience white water are centres with safety provision, including Cardiff International White Water; Holme Pierrepoint National Water Sports Centre near Nottingham, Lee Valley White Water Centre north of London or through Plas y Brenin, the National Centre for Mountain Activities in Snowdonia. There's even a White Water SUP Fest held annually at Mile End Mill White Water Centre, on the Welsh River Dee in Llangollen, North Wales, with workshops and competitions plus camping and evening entertainment.

You could try SUP surfing at Lee Valley White Water Centre, North of London or...

...jack in London for the call of the wild. Glen Etive, West Highlands of Scotland.

This is organised by Stand Up Paddle Board UK, who also provide training throughout the year. Honing your skills on river sections with natural features and curves has a particular appeal.

The group on the big SUP shown on page 211 had previously tackled rapids on Scotland's River Dee, west of Aberdeen. A bit like white water rafting, a megaSup was apparently less likely to get caught in depressions in the surface. These are termed 'stoppers' or more specifically 'holes' and 'hydraulics', where circulating water flows in and can hold a kayak or board. The Dee is another river with a surfable tidal bore wave.

If white water becomes your forte, it is possible to surf by drops, by pointing upstream in circulating water, but this requires a high level of skill and experience, as well as courage!

# Races – speedy boarding!

Races involving sharp turns or some running in and out of the water are known as 'technical' and can be very exciting to watch, let alone compete in. Speed is obviously important, but timing, acceleration and tactics play a huge part, particularly around the turns. Grabbing the inside lane and quick, stable, well-practised manoeuvres can be crucial. If you have the tactical awareness of sailing's Ben Ainslie it can make a significant difference to how well you do.

Manufacturers of boards sometimes help organise sprint events to demonstrate their products. Some clubs practise sprints and it can add a bit of interest to

It can all turn on the turns.

lessons, stag and hen party paddles and school groups. Some centres, such as Bray Lake Watersports in Berkshire, organise various race events, including an annual SUP Clubs Championships. For a purer

Exe Hammer Paddleboard challenge on Devon's River Exe. Perhaps they could also co-ordinate one on the Wye?

*Serious jockeyin' with no gee-gees.*

test of speed, there are straight sprint events on the rowing lake at Holme Pierrepont, the National Water Sports Centre, near Nottingham.

The better known, more promoted race events tend to be longer distances. GBSUP organise various events including a series of five races. These include The Battle of the Thames in London and ones at the White Water Centre in Cardiff and Holme Pierrepont. The series finale is The Battle of the Bay at Sandbanks Beach, Poole, organised with the BaySUP Club, which involves running on the beach with your board

at the start. This is quite an enjoyable spectacle as you can see much of the route from the beach.

A few years ago, I took part in the series' season opening event, known as The Head of the Dart in Devon. This ran from Dartmouth up to Totnes. Both are attractive, interesting cultural towns, which may help when it comes to travel arrangements or making a weekend of it. The race alternates each year between going downstream or upstream with the tide, as it did when I joined the fun. Don't be put off if you're not particularly fit or competitive. There's

**TOP TIP**

Going for an upstream paddle on a fairly swift river will motivate you to keep up a good pace. Take advantage of winter flows to keep your strength and fitness then, when safe to do so. Coastal paddles into a brisk wind will also help.

As they take to the boards the drama unfolds.

a great atmosphere and a wide range of abilities from beginner to winner.

Parking was difficult, so I didn't have time to fully inflate my board. It's good to have an excuse ready, but this makes a fair difference, a bit like riding a bike with flaccid tyres. Most people headed up the middle of the river. Aware that rivers flow fastest between the centre and the outside bend, I tried to keep to the inside of bends once the river had narrowed somewhat. On each straighter stretch several people would overtake, but on each bend I'd end up back in front of some. Further upstream, the flow of the river outweighed the effects of the upcoming tide to a greater extent. With more frequent meanders this strategy became increasingly helpful, until others left me in their wake on the home straight.

Afterwards they have a heart-warming awards ceremony, where the best three in all manner

of categories (inflatable/ rigid, length of board, gender and age) take to a podium. What struck me was that most of those honoured were lighter than average. Like jockeys they had good strength to weight ratios. This is probably to do with heavier folk displacing more water and thus creating more drag.

Tickets sell as fast as Glastonbury music festival. Even if you don't take part or can't book a place in time, races can be very exciting to watch. The fastest in the Dart race come from the 14 foot board Elite Category. In 2019 Hungarian-born Zoltan Erdelyi surged clear of his nearest rivals, Blue Ewer (series winner) and Ryan James, in the home straight to be the winner. The best racers gain sponsorship deals from the top board brands. The fastest female was Marie Buchanan, mentioned below.

Head of the Dart 2019 winner Zoltan Erdelyi after a showery session at Kimmeridge Bay, Dorset.

Ryan James after winning the Battle of the Bay 2019.

Paddle Round the Pier beach festival in Brighton has been going since 1996. It first featured SUP in 2007. With its first SUP endurance race in 2008, it has played its part in promoting the sport as well as raising funds for charity.

For a young sport, there are a fair few bodies actively helping to promote it. UKSUP, who are involved with the Brighton event, also organise the Great Glen Race in Scotland. This features a relatively timid 45km option and a picturesque 92km jaunt taking in the Caledonian Canal, with majestic Loch Ness and two other lochs.

Another monstrous ordeal/team event is the Trent 100 which, unsurprisingly, covers 100km of the River Trent. It began in 2016 and begins at Shugborough Hall, Staffordshire, with participants resting overnight at the intriguing Anchor Caves in Derbyshire and finishing with a party at a festival in Nottingham. It is described as a challenge, not a race, but you must finish within 20 hours. Throwlines and self-releasing waist leashes are a requirement as the early sections can be fast.

For the European sightseer there is the SUP 11 City Tour in the Netherlands, completing around 220km in a gruelling five-day race. Just competing in or completing a race like this brings a great sense of 'winning at life' for many, but for some there are higher goals. In 2013 the event was won by Marie Buchanan, one of our best racers who represents Team GB in the International Surfing Association (ISA) World Championships.

For those wanting to head further afield, you may want to put the epic LA to San Diego Race on your bucket list. It's a long haul of 100 miles (around 160km) along the warm Southern California coast, so think about hydration and drink in the experience. For the faint-hearted it may be done as a relay with teams of up to four people or there's a 50 mile option. Flying with a 14ft race board can be costly, especially if your board suffers damage.

The Association of Paddlesurf Professionals organise the much talked about APP World Tour featuring large events in notable locations, including New York, London, Paris and Osaka. As well as sprint and distance races with the world's top paddlers, these weekend festivals feature other activities from surf to yoga. London even includes litter

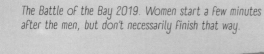

The Battle of the Bay 2019. Women start a few minutes after the men, but don't necessarily finish that way.

Winner Marie Buchanan hotly pursued by a male paddler and second-placed Ginnie Odetayo.

picks with Planet Patrol, so you don't have to be a dedicated athlete to play an important part.

# Race tips

If you want to SUP strongly, SUP weekly (preferably several times)! Various tips can be gleaned from other chapters, such as 'Advanced Techniques' (*see page 30*), but here are a few in distilled form:

- Perfect your paddling technique, with efficient rhythmic flowing movements.
- Racers shorten their stroke and increase their cadence (stroke rate) in a sprint finish, so practise.
- Some move the foot on their upper hand side a little further forward to apply more power.
- Critique your technique – ask someone to film you so you can spot faults or potential improvements.
- Keeping your hands the correct width apart will encourage good form (hold your paddle up with your elbows out at right angles to find this width) – a sticker placed a little lower on your paddle than your lower hand position could help remind you.
- Practise pacing yourself over the distance you'll be racing.
- Eat healthily, with plenty of complex carbohydrates, protein and fresh fruit and vegetables.
- Sleep helps – lack of it can cause fatigue and slower recovery from training.
- Particularly on shorter races, have a pre-race warm-up, possibly paddling gently with perfect technique, limber and, once warm, stretch.
- Train as much as you can, ideally at least four days a week, with some variety and plenty of SUP miles for distance races.
- Ease off the training as race day approaches.
- Plan to arrive at the venue in plenty of time, especially if you've an inflatable board to pump up.

10 • THRILLS, SKILLS AND SPILLS!

- On race days stay hydrated, ideally a sip or two every 15 minutes.
- Don't eat or drink anything you're not used to.
- Enjoy the experience, preferably with friends or family.

SUP racing may make an Olympic appearance before long. It's only a matter of time and a good location before the world's fastest growing watersport arrives on the Olympic stage, so keep practising!

# Multi-discipline events

If you want to try something different, though very mainstream in that it takes place on the Thames between Henley and Marlow, The Hurley Classic is a weekend of paddlesport. Originally a kayak freestyle event since 1989, a SUP race with white water and obstacle course elements has been included in recent years.

For a more varied challenge to your stamina, there are events that take the form of a duathlon or triathlon. Some allow you to perform the different disciplines within a team. Others are completed individually, such as the SUPBIKERUN series. These take place around Britain and the locations vary from year to year, including the Derbyshire Dales, South Wales, Dorset's Isle of Purbeck and Cumbria's Ullswater.

I took part in one in the South Downs. This event began with a 3km SUP zig-zagging across a lake, with starts staggered in small groups. Then there was a mountain bike course of around 30km, including four tough ascents, three of which were off-road, followed by a 5km run to round it off nicely. After the paddling and pedalling, my legs felt stiff for the whole run. The last 500m were on a path almost alongside the busy A27. As I finally reached this, I've never been so pleased to find myself running near a major road.

Generally it was well organised with numbered stickers and labels for all your kit. One slight disappointment in that event was that there was no hullabaloo for the top finishers, not that this applied to me. A phenomenally fit friend was the fastest female overall, despite falling in on the final turn of the SUP and completing the cycle and run with a very wet bum.

SUP can also support charities. This photo was taken at the River Itchen, Southampton, at one of several 'SUP for Cancer' events.

*It's the taking part, particularly on the podium!*

# Boards for specific activities

Various features will make a board more fit for purpose, particularly the dimensions and shape.

**Size summary for different uses:**

| Use | Size |
|-----|------|
| All-purpose | 9'6" to 11'6" × 30" to 34" |
| Touring | 11' to 12'  × 32" to 39" |
| Racing | 12'6" to 15' × 22" to 30" |
| White water | 9' to 10'6" × 32" to 35" |
| Surfing | 6'6" to 10' × 26" to 32" |

Displacement hull for racing.

Racing boards, as well as being long and narrow, have the most pointed noses for cutting through the water. The best ones are rigid and they may also have a displacement hull. This means when viewed from the front, the underside of the front of the board curves down to a point in the middle like a racing rowing boat. This becomes a smooth curve further back to minimise friction. These are less stable, but also help to part the water. The more specialist designs with very narrow widths are more for the expert. Racers sometimes fall when turning and need good balance. The narrowest boards are better for flat water, with more stable variations for sea racing.

Multi-person race SUPs are known as 'dragon boards'. At the Head of the Dart

## BOARD SHAPES AND SIZES

Board shapes vary somewhat but are along these lines. Some boards will be less pointed at the back or 'tail'. SUP surfboards may have blunt but rounded noses like an all-purpose board or more pointed ones. Racing and white water may have higher rails.

All purpose

Touring

Race

White water

Surf

Race a few years ago there was a very long thin board, which three people rode on very effectively; it created quite a wake as it surged past me at the start. There were four valves, any of which could be used for inflation, though while two of its participants went off to register, one poor individual was left to pump. Several teams of four people now race the event on Red Paddle Co. Dragon boards, which are 22 feet long.

Racing aside, most boards have a flatter base, sometimes known as a planing hull, designed to skim over the water. They still displace water unless you catch a surf wave and glide over the surface more. The highest speeds used when touring wouldn't tend to exceed 8 mph whereas 20 mph could be reached when surfing. Touring boards, though much wider for stability and carrying dry-bags, also have pointed noses for efficiency.

Boards for SUP surfing will often narrow toward the front, as well as being narrower at the back and less deep than touring boards. They will tend to have more of a 'rocker', so when viewed from the side there will be more of a curve underneath to give more stability and manoeuvrability in waves. Instead of stubbing into waves with a jolt, boards with more rocker will help you ride over them, though they won't be as fast. Some surfboards are particularly curved up at the back. Being shorter they are more responsive to pivoting hips and turning strokes. Rigid boards can have a much more tailored design, though inflatables can have extra moulded material on the sides. Some ISUPs for surfing are only 4" thick, which can help with turning.

White water boards, be they inflatable or rigid, will need to be very robust. If they are wider with higher rails (sides) it will make them more stable, particularly when applying pressure on the downstream side, then the opposite way when crossing into an eddy. (Some race boards have high rails for stability also.) They tend to be short for manoeuvrability, particularly those intended for playing and surfing drops, rather than progressing down a river run. A sharp nose would take some tough punishment so theirs are more curved as well. They also feature a fair amount of rocker. They need good deck grip and a raised back edge will help prevent slipping off the back.

All-purpose boards tend to be more curved at the front, but this is good for beginners as they're

Surfing a race board could be useful at the end of a coastal contest.

*A more shaped fin.*

robust and stable. They will have more rocker than a touring board, so they are better for practising skills like step back turns. If you live inland you may prefer a compromise between a touring board and an all-purpose board.

The other important design feature is the fin or fins. Touring and racing boards tend to have one removable fin. Being removable helps with packing as well as allowing you to swap fins or alter the position. Most are shaped pretty much like a dolphin's dorsal, though some specialist fins have a more shaped back edge. Fins help with 'tracking' or steering control.

Having the fin further back will improve tracking (staying straight) slightly, so you don't have to change sides or do such pronounced bow strokes. It will also make the board a little faster. A pike's dorsal fin is set far back for sudden bursts of speed. Being further forward will allow easier turns. The more surface area, the more stability it gives.

Some surf shops sell a wide range of fins, which cost from £15 to £100 or more. Plastic fins are durable, whereas some other materials such as fibreglass will be more breakable. However, it is better to break the fin than the housing or 'US fin-box' it comes in. The fin is usually secured with a small inexpensive square nut and bolt. Some boards have specific fins that slip into them securely. If they're difficult to remove, they may be easier with the board deflated and lubricant, such as WD40, helps. Starboard have developed ones that simply squeeze into place with small rollers, which are becoming the norm. Make sure you put fins in with the bottom edge pointing backward like a dolphin's!

Designs featuring two or more shorter, more swept back fins are generally preferred for white water and surfing. White water boards have various fin arrangements, sometimes four or more. Removable fins can be changed to suit the features of the river and can be easily replaced if broken. The classic Red inflatable 10'6" all-round board comes with three fixed plastic fins. These can become temporarily a little bent in packing but can be straightened with warm water or a hair-dryer. The advantage is that they're tough and there's no fitting required, just pump and go. All-purpose boards may have one or three fins.

*Humpback whale tail fin.*
*'Call that flap on your board a fin?'*

# 11 BODY AND SOUL

SUP to stay youthful.

# SUP for a healthier life

New skills and challenges stimulate your brain. Learning to stand-up paddle and develop your technique will do this and improve your balance. It may mean a few tumbles in water, but less likelihood of falls and injury from these in later life.

On hot days it's easy to cool off, deliberately or otherwise, and there are many benefits to an outdoor dip, particularly in saltwater, which is good for your immune system, sinuses and skin. Cold water stimulates the metabolism and your white blood cells. Regular outdoor swimmers rarely catch colds.

Frequent physical activity can reduce blood pressure and your cholesterol ratio, as well as the chances of developing type 2 diabetes and certain cancers including colon and breast. Supping is particularly good for troublesome areas like knees and backs. By keeping your knees at least slightly bent, they act as shock absorbers. Being a low-impact, non-contact exercise it shouldn't create physical injuries. The resistance of the water will strengthen your bones and muscles, putting the fizz into your physique.

SUP is a wonderful way to alleviate stress. The physical aspect works off the frustrations of the day, while communing with nature massages the deeper reaches of your mental well-being. A few minutes paddling on a river or lying on a gently rocking board on the sea or a rippled lake can help you to forget you have the boss from Hell. Advocates of 'Mindfulness' relieve stress by focusing on their awareness of the feeling beneath their feet. Few activities rely on foot feelings to the same extent as standing on a paddleboard, soothing from soles to soul.

SUP solitude, Pembrokeshire.

# Nutrition

Fresh fruit and vegetables, especially bright coloured ones like blueberries and beetroot, will help to replace vitamins and minerals lost through the exertions and perspiration of a seasoned Supper. Bananas, tomatoes, citrus fruits and leafy greens are good sources of potassium. Known as an electrolyte, this helps maintain a healthy fluid balance. While paddling, you may have the opportunity to pick blackberries that are too high for kayakers and inaccessible to walkers, but they're not worth scratching your board for.

Fresh mackerel, possibly caught from a SUP, is an excellent source of protein to aid muscle recovery, but also omega 3 which will keep your joints lubricated. Vegetarian sources include flax and chia seeds, which give your joints more omega bounce per ounce than mackerel, and are a preferable addition to smoothies!

If you like foraging food for free, look out for the orange berries and thin grey/green leaves of sea buckthorn, which is often found on the coast. The berries, which can be eaten raw or made into juice, are rich in several omega oils including omega 3 and various vitamins. They have a distinctive sharp taste and sharper thorns. Fortunately they also benefit your eyesight, which will aid you in spotting these. If you forget the sunscreen, you can even rub the juice on skin to help prevent sunburn. Its beneficial oils also keep your colon and bowels healthily lubricated, so you may want to go steady on long paddles.

All foods, even healthy ones, should only be eaten in moderation. Be it beetroot, blueberries, blackberries or buckthorn, don't go bananas on any food!

## Fuelling for gruelling

If you've a demanding day's Supping ahead of you, such as a long race or tour it may be worth thinking about your food intake. If the race will last around an hour

*Supping gives you the opportunity to enjoy an epic picnic in beautiful surroundings.*

Sea buckthorn.

or less, the best policy is to stick to your usual, hopefully healthy diet. If it's a bit more demanding or your tour is longer than you're used to, make sure you eat plenty of complex 'carbs' the day before, but not too late if it tends to affect your sleep. Good options include potatoes, sweet potatoes, wholegrain cereals, rice and pasta.

Cereal bars can be a good boost of energy and carbohydrate to help with endurance. Opt for those made with dried fruit over ones with glucose/fructose syrup. If you want to have control over the ingredients and save money you could: *make your own kind of muesli and bake your own special bars.*

It's best not to try high energy snack bars or gels on a race day if you're not used to them. They may affect your stomach and if you wolf them too fast you could get indigestion. You could try them sometimes while training lightly over a period of time.

Don't eat anything too heavy during the day. You might feel your packed lunch lacked punch, but it's better than feeling as if you've been hit in the stomach every time you stretch for a paddle stroke!

After a challenge listen to your body, it could be feeling sensitive after all the exertion. Dietitian and regular Supper Sarah Alicea suggests a large glass of milk, or a chicken or humous sandwich.

# Hydration

Dehydration is not unusual among Suppers and particularly instructors. You may be in a warm wetsuit. You're active, but don't always get chance to drink. You're also aware that you may not get a chance to relieve yourself and some locations lack toilets. In some ways it can be harder for women.

One way to see whether you're drinking enough is to check the colour of your urine. If it's clear or light straw-coloured you're fine, but dark yellow means your kidneys are struggling. The best way to help is to drink plenty of water, little and often. Gulping can trap air and is less likely to be absorbed into your body so well.

Some people carry a 'camelback' to sip on, consisting of a small backpack of water with a drinking tube. Some find them uncomfortable or tend not to sip enough. You may prefer a hydration pack

A water bottle cover with a Velcro strap keeps water cool and handy.

*For fabulous 'abs' and glorious 'glutes'*
*Supping is abso-blooming-lutely brilliant!*

that fits around your waist like a bum-bag. A company called Vaikobi produce a buoyancy aid with an in-built hydration pack. For tours I attach a water bottle to my board using a cover with a Velcro strap, but it disrupts your rhythm to use it in a race. This wouldn't be wise in a mucky waterway. While teaching I sometimes keep a small bottle in my buoyancy aid pocket. You can keep spare water or other drinks in a dry-bag.

Many drinks are diuretic, meaning they make you less hydrated by the time you've flushed them out. Alcohol, some fizzy drinks and caffeine drinks tend to come into this category.

Sports drinks contain similar dilutions of sugars and salts as our own body fluid. They are termed 'isotonic' and are absorbed into the gut slightly faster than water. They contain a fair few calories which can give you energy, but drunk regularly might affect your teeth and your waistline. In a race of less than an hour

they probably won't bring gains, but could make a difference in longer lasting events. However, as with food, don't take them on a race day unless you've got used to them and you know they won't give you any problems. You don't want to experience turbulence when facilities may be in greater demand than supply!

# Fitness

One of the best ways to train for paddleboarding is, of course, plenty of paddling – toning your physique while honing your technique. Once mastered, it exercises the many muscles in your feet and most of the ones from there up to your head. It is particularly good for your core. Being a good all-round workout, Supping is also excellent 'cross-training' for other activities and it's good to vary your exercise.

One winter I'd been doing 'Parkrun' 5km runs and my times had stopped improving. In the summer I was too busy paddling, including teaching, tours and race training. When I resumed Parkrun in the autumn, despite hardly any running in between, my times were about a minute faster. This was presumably due to the benefits regular paddling has for your heart, lungs and general fitness.

Although you may not be able to imagine being 'paddle-bored', some days you may want to give your SUP muscles a rest, or the weather may be too windy. Doing a variety of other activities, such as swimming, cycling and exercise classes can improve your fitness for Supping.

## SUP fitness classes

There are fitness classes done on the water with boards, preferably inflatable ones. These vary from being more like SUP Yoga, which will be described later, to circuit training mixed with Supping. This

Using a weighted rope will strengthen many muscles used in Supping.

might involve varied races and relays or alternating between exercises like sit ups or press ups on a board and paddling.

Some exercises like 'burpees', which are a combination of press ups, squat thrusts and jumps, come with a fair probability of falling off. Repeatedly climbing back on is a demanding workout in itself, but it can make it difficult to know what to wear on evenings when the water isn't so warm. Wetsuits are fairly restrictive, so I prefer

SUP fitness class.

*Raft race.*

running kit. You could wear a couple of layers. Try not to fall off early on or you'll have to work particularly hard to stay warm. Later in the class you can risk doing star jumps, tuck jumps or burpees more boldly.

With a few friends you could make up your own classes and exercises. Leashing two boards together and taking it in turns to tow is a good way to increase resistance. Don't both paddle against each other or you may damage the leash or board loop.

Some swimming pools are now offering 'float fit' classes, inspired by SUPs. Participants perform fitness and Yoga exercises while balanced on large floats in pools. Water aerobics classes also provide a generally low impact workout, though men should beware the buoyancy of foam 'noodles', which can rise suddenly, delivering a low blow with a high impact!

# Exercises to help you SUP

The stronger you are, the less effort paddling will take and power can improve your speed. If you have access to a gym there are usually a variety of exercise machines to tone or strengthen the major muscles used in Supping. There's a need for a SUP-simulator with a screen showing virtual environments. On slower settings, images of river or marine life could enhance a warm-up, a warm down or simply warm the cockles of your heart.

Exercises are a good way to keep or build your strength over the winter when you're spending less time out on the water. If you have someone to train with it can make it more enjoyable and you can motivate each other. Stop if you feel back pain. Some exercises require

*Races can make the lungs blow and laughs flow.*

*Try a full minute of plank or two short planks!*

*Even press ups can be a fun challenge!*

*Exercising in pairs can provide extra resistance and more enjoyment.*

*Trying variations on a board can add excitement.*

no equipment, some will give you a hard core and some are only for the hardcore fitness fanatic. Popular ones include leg raises, 'ab crunches, plank, side plank and torso raises. Press ups are particularly good for paddlers and will even help you pump up inflatables!

There are many exercises with a pair of small weights or dumbbells. With some

you can add extra weight should you wish to. Start with fairly light weights and do sets of 10 repetitions. Here are a few that will add power to your paddling:

Lie on your back on a mat, carpet or exercise bench with your knees slightly raised and weights in each hand. These will tone and strengthen your pectoral muscles:

*Renegade press ups.*

*Increase your weights gradually over time or do more repetitions.*

1 **Lift the weights up** in front of you like an upside down press up action. Lifting them alternately will be more akin to Supping, with a slightly greater range of movement.

2 **In the upside down** press up position with elbows a little bent, rotate the weights in small circles in opposite directions above your chest.

3 **For your shoulders** and back assume the press up position, but with dumbbells in your hands, bring one weight up to your shoulder a bit like a rowing action, then lower that one and raise the other. Alternate one with each weight with press ups. These are known as 'renegade press ups'. They are hard, but much easier resting on your knees than on your toes.

A very useful piece of equipment that isn't particularly expensive is a pull up bar. Different grips, such as wide or narrow and fingers facing toward you or away,

*Different arm positions strengthen different muscles.*

*Leg raises help keep you svelte below the belt.*

# Warming up

Before a SUP session it is a good idea to limber up. This will warm the muscles, tendons and ligaments, preparing them for action and reducing the risk of injury. It is especially important on colder days or after a long car journey. This can be done on arrival, as a break from pumping up your board or after a brief jog or brisk walk on the beach or up and down steps.

As Supping is an all-round exercise, you want to activate all the major muscles. Done with others it can be fun. Try not to feel self-conscious; it's beneficial. Though on your own you may want to avoid the likes of pelvic thrusts. Just do around six repetitions of each, repeating asymmetric ones on each side alternately. There are various options but here are a few to try between reading (unless you're on a train!):

will tone different upper body and arm muscles. Raising your knees is a great way to tone your abdominal muscles, particularly the lower ones, without straining your back.

A Swiss ball or exercise ball can also be used for many exercises, particularly to strengthen your core. With care you can also kneel on top of them, which is good for your core stability and balance. Gyms sometimes have half balls known as Bosu balls (they aren't cheap). Squatting on the flat side (curved side down) will strengthen your legs and stabilise your knees as well as test your balance. Side-stepping between the curved sides of two Bosu balls will have similar benefits.

To keep your legs springy, strong and stable — select squats!

Flowing side stretches.

1 **Legs** – squatting activates your leg and buttock muscles, including the largest muscles - your quadriceps (thighs), so it is a good one to begin with. As you spring up bring your elbows back to stretch your chest too. Keep your back straight and look ahead.

2 **Shoulders** – rotate your arms a few times forward and a greater number backward as this helps with posture also.

3 **Back** – swing one arm around in front of you and twist your torso around this way as you swing your other arm around your back. It is important to raise the knee on the front arm side to avoid twisting it.

4 **Sides** – swing one arm from the side over your head as you swing the other sideways across in front of your hips while moving your hip outward on the upper arm side in a flowing action.

## Stretching

Having warmed your muscles, they deserve a good stretch to prepare them for the activity to come. This helps to align the muscles correctly and reduces the risk of injury. Muscle fibres are somewhat elastic. Once they've had a good controlled stretch they are less likely to be 'pulled', so hopefully you shouldn't miss out on paddling opportunities.

The next section on SUP Yoga may provide more enlightenment when it comes to stretching, particularly the list of maxims. Stretch as far as you're comfortable, but don't strain – it's not a competitive sport. Hopefully you will feel the muscles ease after a short while in the stretch, which may take anything from 10 seconds to over a minute. Then you can try to increase the stretch on an out breath.

A handful of positions that stretch the main muscles to be used is worth the time. At the end of the SUP session try to warm down rather than suddenly stopping after a sprint. Then have another good old set of stretches. This will help to strengthen

*Once warm, muscles love a good stretch.*

*'Come up one vertebra at a time', preferably in the right order!*

*You stretch my back, I'll stretch yours.*

# SUP Yoga – how SUP'll keep you supple!

Yoga has been practised in India for millennia, and in the West for many decades for the physical and mental benefits it brings. Indoor yoga classes involve bending, stretching, twisting, balancing and breathing exercises, movements and postures, done in a relaxed or somewhat meditative state of mind. It improves posture, muscle tone and the health of your internal organs.

SUP Yoga incorporates traditional yoga techniques, but can be a little different, offering more of a challenge. It can be a powerful combination bringing the benefits of both disciplines. Trying to remain in control of a board will place greater demands on your muscles, particularly your core, than yoga on a mat. It may be less spiritual and often

and lengthen your muscles, reducing the chances of them tightening up and feeling stiff.

A classic stretch is touching your toes which works your back, shoulders, arms, buttocks and hamstrings. Once comfortable, let the weight of your arms increase the stretch on an out breath. Don't bounce down. I've heard a few yoga teachers suggest 'Come back up one vertebra at a time'. This sounds like a physical challenge for the most accomplished yogi, but they mean think of each one as you come up slowly, starting with the lower ones. Finish by stretching your arms high above your head.

*They're all about that base! Boards may be anchored, tied to a rope or fitted to a base.*

233

*Reflective yoga in Barcelona.*

more fun. Participants are surrounded by fresh air and sometimes find themselves immersed, not just in the moment but in fresh or salty water.

Sooner or later the instructor won't be able to resist including a pose that involves balance. This could be the 'warrior' pose which involves lunging, with your arms outstretched or above your head, and a lot of concentration. Harder still is the 'tree' pose: placing one foot against the inside of the other standing leg with your hands together. If the class didn't involve balance it wouldn't really embrace being on a board on water.

As the session leader continues in their mellow tones, someone is almost bound to fall in and the meditative atmosphere is interrupted with splashing and laughter. If the person who falls doesn't topple their neighbours too, the wave created as they clamber back on will present a further challenge. A whole domino effect may ensue.

Personally I think it's best to try not to fall so you develop balance, but still go whole-heartedly for the best positions (known as 'asanas', pronounced 'ass-er-ners') you can, without being inhibited. Instructors almost certainly won't mind. That's part of the experience and what makes it different to a traditional class. Once someone succumbs to the ancient art of unintentionally falling in water, everyone will feel more relaxed, particularly if it's the teacher who takes a tumble!

*Not waving but stretching.*

One way to entertain and relax your class.

Seeing things from a different angle can help build bridges.

It can be difficult to know how to dress. A full wetsuit can feel a bit restrictive, though ideally you don't want to feel cold or worry about falling in. Classes don't normally go ahead unless the weather is mild and calm. They generally last an hour or just 30 minutes. On a warm day when the water isn't too cold, most people wouldn't wear a wetsuit. A long john wetsuit (bare shoulders), a 'shortie' or a very flexible modern one are options.

Fitting a little yoga in at the end of other SUP sessions when you're warmed up is a good idea. This can also provide a beneficial, perhaps meditative, cool down after the exercise of Supping. Practising yoga without a board obviously helps.

Try to keep the asanas balanced. Always do the same on both sides of the body, but also alternate between backward bends and forward bends. If you do a job that involves bending forward a lot, you may want to dwell more on back stretches that reverse this.

A few other maxims to bear in mind:

● Warm up and do gentle stretches before trying demanding ones.
● Stretch more as you breathe out.
● Try to hold positions for at least 30 seconds.

Lakes make good yoga venues.

● You can do a stretch then ease off briefly before increasing the stretch.
● Stop if anything feels wrong or too painful/uncomfortable.
● It can help to imagine a beautiful scene such as a gorgeous beach or peaceful lake, but in SUP Yoga you may not have to imagine.
● Think about the muscles you're stretching and toning with each asana, along with the benefits to your endocrine glands which may be harder to visualise!

Here are a few of the most practised:

Supine.

Warrior.

Peacock.

Child.

Shoulder stand.

Twisting.

Bow.

Plough.

Purvottanasana.

236

*Walk your feet toward your face until you feel they have to lift up.*

The SUPine pose was too appropriate to leave out and works wonders for all manner of glands and organs. Asanas have Sanskrit names, though English names may be easier for Westerners to remember, with the possible exception of purvottanasana or upward plank pose.

One of the most beneficial is the brain-boosting, age-reversing headstand or sirshasana. It involves walking your feet toward your head until you feel they have to come up, but it can be done in different ways.

*The greatest asana and on a hard board!*

- Holding the sides of your board helps balance.
- Making a triangle with your forearms and placing your hands around your head gives a little more neck support.
- No hands or 'break dance' style. If you want the 'wow', it is the greatest asana!

## TOP TIP

The twisting pose, vakrasana, will keep your spine supple and improve your twist turns!

# 12 WHAT'S UP?
## The social side

Supping can be a wonderful way to make new friends and socialise. It's very conducive to chatting, people feel relaxed and there's often plenty of things around you to converse about. A SUP community is developing. The length and breadth of Britain, organised groups, with a shared passion for paddling, are forming or already established.

Supping makes a great team building activity with colleagues.

# Groups

These may be co-ordinated by companies teaching skills, watersport retailers or just people wanting to begin a group in their area. If you're fairly new to SUP the first two options are good ways to try different boards and receive tuition, either informally on tours or through classes and courses. Other groups are great if you have some experience and your own equipment. Activities are often promoted through social media such as Facebook and WhatsApp.

Some clubs may have a regular meeting place, such as a particular beach or a riverside pub. The pub may help host the group so they can benefit from any traditional supping after Supping. Board hire could be a good sideline for pubs. Other groups may try to vary their locations and their thirst-quenching socials. A SUP games session can add variety. North Hants SUP have even acquired 'pugil sticks'.

Groups are sprouting up like dandelions. If there isn't one gathering within easy reach, perhaps you could start your own? It will take some planning on a regular basis, but welcoming new people and bringing enjoyment to your gang can be very satisfying. A steady flow of new

Paddle to a pub, Wareham, Dorset.

Sup New Forest Group, near Hurst Spit.

Paddle picnic.

Who'll stand for chairperson?

'How long can you count on me?'

your next 'board meeting'! Meeting up with other clubs can be a great way to enjoy the best paddles in another area and Supping is a very friendly activity.

Sometimes Supper couples will form through these groups, which may give you a warm feeling inside, but might reduce their availability, especially if families follow. Watersport providers have been known to organise 'Singles SUPs' or SUP speed-dating. Paddling can be a relaxed informal way to break the ice and maybe meet a partner or make for a great date. Pack a picnic and SUP through the sunset!

members keeps groups interesting and may help to maintain a spread of ages. Alternatively, you could restrict the club to 'by invite only' so it is more manageable.

It would be advisable to look into insurance and worth checking access is OK for your paddles. As a group you may have more issues but in some places it could give you more chance of permission, especially if you offer to litter-pick or do other good deeds. With friends you can do a recce of potential paddles. Hopefully other members will help and come up with suggestions for

' ... Till the sun dries up the sea.'

*Race-goers on tour, Brownsea Island.*

# Forums, views and news

When you're not perfecting your paddle stroke, one way to learn more about SUP is to look at online forums (*see page 253*). You can pick up tips, ask for advice and read opinions – sometimes several differing ones. If you're looking for a group in your area or a recommendation of where to SUP if visiting another region or country, you can post an enquiry.

Manufacturers like Red and Fanatic have news and stories on their websites, as do some retailers. From the US, a particularly readable one is *Pumped UP SUP*. There are also UK-based magazines and their websites, including *SUP International* and *SUP Mag UK*; both publish broad-ranging articles, interviews and equipment reviews. Other worldwide options in print or online are *Stand Up Journal*, *SUP World Mag*, *SUPboarder* (*online*) *SUP Passion* (online) and not forgetting *SUP Connect*. They often feature inspiring travel suggestions. When you're suffering from paddle withdrawal symptoms on wet winter weekends or dark dank evenings you can at least dream of, plan or book your next SUP session to satisfy what may become a healthy obsession.

# Events

It's always good to have something to look forward to and the paddleboard calendar benefits from a variety of appealing events to dip your toes into. Race events provide opportunities to meet people and explore the area. After the Battle of the Bay race in 2019, I led a tour around Brownsea Island in Poole Harbour of around 10km. Those that had just taken part in the 14km race off the beach, on a hot day, earned my respect, including the oldest competitor, aged 71.

SUP Armada event, Bewl Water, Kent.

Races have been described in the 'Thrills, Skills and Spills' chapter but there are also charity fundraisers and festivals. Often representatives of equipment manufacturers and retailers take the opportunity to raise their profiles and let people see their wares.

I've worked at a few of these, including Poole Watersports Festival weekend organised by H2O, the National Watersports Festival at Hayling Island, and the SUP Armada at Bewl Water in Kent. Southern England has its fair share, perhaps more, but there are others and some events vary their locations. Some offer taster sessions in paddling and SUP Yoga. Trade stands will be there to offer expert advice, demonstrate the latest advances in kit as well as letting you try a wide range of equipment in the hope that you'll buy.

The SUP Armada is a charity fundraiser and the UK's largest festival specialising in paddleboarding. To give the event extra focus they try to break the world record for the most people paddling a route at one time. I was asked to lead the way by Andy Gratwick of Easyriders, who was one of the main organisers. I got myself primed and ready with my board on the shoreline, but there was a bit of toing and froing while the buoys were moved into place to mark the course and I tried to

The trip begins.

make sure I knew the route I'd be taking with hundreds following. When the hooter sounded I leapt into action but didn't realise my leash had ended up caught around my unleashed ankle. I nearly went head first, cheeks over chest into the water.

It had been a gorgeous day with the temperature over 30° and a massive turnout. Fortunately I just managed to hop free of my leash and regain my balance before the event photographer, Dave White, caught the moment I set off. A mass pile-up was avoided and the record of 390 Suppers paddling a mile course was successfully officially set.

Local groups often have smaller events, possibly involving a picnic or barbecue. They may go somewhere further afield than usual, such as a camping or surfing trip. Certain dates in the year can provide a theme. I've done a couple of Halloween paddles appropriately dressed. When a youngster became blown off course, it felt strange

The *Guardian magazine*'s Santa SUP cover by Fabio De Paola, with kind permission from *The Guardian*.

dashing across to check on him while dressed as a wizard with my hat threatening to fly off.

Having a Santa SUP has become a tradition with some groups and a good way to work off a few excesses in the festive season. One year with Easyriders we did a photo shoot for the *Guardian* newspaper's Christmas magazine supplement, which graced the front cover as well as accompanying a feature inside. We carefully spent about an hour trying to position ourselves for Fabio the photographer without nudging boards and knocking each other off: no ho-ho-hoing matter in winter. Stuffing my Santa suit with padding including my trusty buoyancy aid didn't help with balance but kept me safe and warm on a chilly day.

I've a terrible feeling this was my fault!

## Organising events

You or your group may decide to organise your own event. Initial things to think about are:

- **What is its purpose** – helping charities, raising group funds, attracting new members, enthusing people about SUP.
- **Who is it aimed at** – just your group, families, potential new members, anyone?
- **Location/venue** – necessary permissions (landowner, local authority, coastguard), potential hazards
- **Will it have a theme** or focus, particular activities, a finale?
- **How big will it be?**

If it's a fairly small affair it might not take much organising, but anything more involved needs careful planning. It could grow to become a regular highlight on the SUP calendar.

## Teaching

Teaching may take various forms, from leading a challenging group tour to letting a couple of friends take turns at giving it a try with one board.

This may seem a slightly strange chapter for a section on teaching, but when the components of other chapters like 'The Elements' and 'Equipment' are behaving well, teaching SUP is a very enjoyable way of bringing people together.

If you're running a class, by including a social element, such as bringing fruit or even homemade muesli bars, it gives people more chance to chat. This can bond your group together like the egg in an omelette, to stick with the food theme.

As a teacher, you have certain aims and responsibilities which can be summed up with the initials SEA:

*Hen do high jinks.*

- **Safety** – vitally important.
- **Enjoyment** – SUP should bring fun.
- **Ability** – people should feel you've helped them to increase their ability and gained a sense of **achievement**.

When the conditions are less well behaved it's a harder job, but with good planning, experience and sometimes quick thinking, the instructor can help to ensure and achieve all the elements of SEA.

Another acronym that can be used in teaching and communicating is EMI:

- **Entertaining**
- **Memorable**
- **Informative**

That's how it should be. If it isn't entertaining and memorable, the informative aspect will be a waste of time. Obviously it's a balance, which will vary from group to group. It can be a mistake to try to be too entertaining. Hopefully that balance hasn't been too bad in this book, even if the attempts at humour have been woeful. If you have a sound enjoyable plan with room for some adaptability, it should be all right. Discuss or communicate major changes to the plan with other leaders, if possible, perhaps by radio.

I spent five years lecturing on countryside recreation and various aspects of nature conservation. I soon found there's more to teaching than knowing your subject and getting it across well. You have to encourage the less confident ones and help people who learn best in different ways. Empathy is particularly important. Taking a moment to put yourself in their shoes (or neoprene footwear) will help you to help them.

To some extent the emphasis will depend on the group and you may have to gauge this when they arrive. With birthday parties, families or groups of

*The splash before the hen do bash.*

referring to their son, firmly whisper to her husband 'Let it go' in frosty, if not frozen, tones. I hope they all had a good holiday.

If you want to do any significant teaching, there are courses leading to qualifications. I took BSUPA's Level 1 and 2 courses, with Andy Gratwick (BSUPA Head Coach). Even if I hadn't become an instructor, I felt that the courses taught me an enormous amount, made me think and gave me confidence in the sport. If you are considering teaching, taking as much relevant training as you can would be highly recommended. Other bodies also run courses, including those for canoeing and for surfing, such as ISA and ASI, as does the Water Skills Academy. First aid and safety tuition is also very important.

Fitness instructor courses can also give a useful grounding in a range of relevant learning, especially if you're taking SUP fitness classes. I took an online Level 3 Fitness Diploma with 32 modules ranging from physiology to finance.

As a SUP instructor it can be well worth trying to work with more than one organisation, especially ones with different clientele, to broaden your experience and potentially increase your work opportunities. SUP combines well with teaching other activities, particularly wind-reliant sports for breezier days. Companies tend to balance SUP provision with at least one wind-based pastime such as kitesurfing to embrace different weathers.

Commercial insurance is a requirement

youngsters there may be more emphasis on fun with games, races and challenges. Hen and stag parties may want a tour with a little malarkey, though the shameless shenanigans tend to come after the Supping. It will be somewhat different with a bunch of experienced adults who are hoping to see a kingfisher. Managing expectations is important. Try not to build up hopes that might not materialise. An otter is unlikely to interact with you, especially when there are several of you in a group.

The personalities within a group can lead to the biggest challenges for the instructor. This can be particularly the case with families, though the vast majority are friendly and wonderful to work with. One holidaying family of four all stood up well quite early on, until the front of the boy's board unintentionally and very gently nudged the back of his dad's, causing a dramatic fall. The father wouldn't stop sternly criticising him. Toward the end I was distracting the father with friendly chat when his daughter shot into the back of my board. While remounting, I overheard Mum,

if taking money. If people are under 18 there may be other considerations and the Adventure Activities Licensing Service (AALS) should be contacted. (Licences aren't normally required if a parent or legal guardian is present.)

# Nurturing novices

The good thing about teaching beginners is that they haven't formed any bad habits. *Novices have no vices!*

Remembering information from earlier chapters, particularly 'Basic Techniques', a plan for teaching complete beginners could be:

1 **Cheerfully welcome them** as they arrive and give out wetsuits, if needed, and buoyancy aids.

2 **Let them know where** they can change, leave bags, etc.

3 **Give out paddles** adjusted for length.

4 **Ask them to form a semi-circle** around a board the right way up balanced across an upturned board, with you on the upwind side of them.

5 **Introduce yourself** and any other staff to the group and, if there are 12 or fewer, ask them to call out their names. Try to remember at least a few for now.

6 **Tell them the plan,** explaining whether it has to be flexible, ask them to stay as a group, state any limits and inform

of any hazards. Let them know what to do if they start being blown away: step off if shallow, or kneel or prone paddle to shore or back to the group, depending on the conditions or plan. One instructor may stay at the back. Ask whether they have questions. Say whether you will use a whistle and what they should do if you do.

7 **Show them the board,** mention the leash, demonstrate strokes, demonstrate standing – emphasise look ahead, explain the way around the paddle goes and how to cope with waves or other local features.

8 **Have them try swapping** hand positions for paddling on both the left and right.

9 **Give them another chance** to ask you any questions.

10 **Give out boards,** appropriate to their size if possible, reminding them to leash before entering the water.

Try to speak clearly, and check they can hear you. Don't talk too fast, but keep

*'Your paddle goes wrist height.'*

247

it brief, unless you're waiting for the tide or equipment to come back. Ask questions to involve them and reinforce learning such as 'where do you look as you stand up?'. Use eye contact. Wearing sunglasses prevents this, though the sun and its reflection can affect your vision. A hat will help with glare, make you recognisable and protect your head from the sun.

Let them get used to strokes, including turning, while on their knees. As people become ready, demonstrate standing on the water (well, on a board now you're on the water!). Help strugglers, talk them through it and hold their board steady if required. You could tell them you found it hard at first.

Praise the good points. Exercise class instructors tend to be brilliant at correcting faults without picking on people. Tell someone audibly that their posture is good or that they're getting their paddle blade well into the water, in preference to yelling to the person nearby that they're doing it wrong. Humour can help and people tend to prefer a constructive witticism to criticism.

Amiable conversation relaxes people, though don't talk from behind to a standing beginner, they may fall off. I often ask if they do any other sports. This may give an indication as to their stamina, strength or balance. Once comfortable, encourage them to deliberately wobble their boards to test their balance and reflexes.

Save bow strokes and bow cross turns for another lesson or later in the first session with quick learners. Stepping off your board and guiding their hands can really help with these.

# Supporting Suppers with special needs

Supping is wonderful for mental health and great therapy for some physical injuries. Apparently nearly 14 million people in the UK have what could be described as some form of disability. There are many varied special needs. For instance, something as specific as visual impairment can encompass a wide range of conditions to different degrees.

Some people with particular sensory issues naturally compensate with their other senses, which may help with some aspects of SUP. Hearing aids may need to be removed before going on the water, so some knowledge of sign language and keeping your face visible will help where people have impaired hearing.

Some watersports, such as sailing, have a long history of creating opportunities for people with different needs. Although you can kneel or sit on SUPs and some have back rests, the extra support offered by some canoes and sit-on-top kayaks may make them more obvious choices for people with some physical disabilities. Some wheelchair-users can paddle a SUP board in a kneeling position with minimal help. Fitting an outrigger to a board would increase stability, or two boards could be connected together.

Wide SUPs with high rails, such as those used for white water, are very stable. If these can be fitted with chairs, it will afford people an open raised position. Landing areas can be adapted to allow wheelchairs onto stable buoyant SUPs designed for the purpose, though serious difficulties that could conceivably occur on the water need careful consideration. A company called Mere Mountains has taken people in wheelchairs on a megaSup from Fell Foot Park on Lake Windermere. The National Trust have endeavoured to provide accessible facilities here and elsewhere.

The British Canoeing website shows the locations of 'Paddle Ability Centres', though some may be more canoe and kayak oriented. Choice of location, particularly with non-swimmers, and the need for good conditions can make organising more of a challenge. The risk assessment would have to be water tight, for want of a better phrase. Supping is thought to be the fastest growing outdoor sport in the US, according to their Outdoor Industries Association. Some providers in America work hard to include people with different challenges and we need to share knowledge and imaginative solutions in this regard.

As a teacher, many people will need you to be particularly patient, supportive and encouraging. Techniques such as holding the board as students try standing, and parallel paddling to help with steering, can be very useful. Where people struggle to move into the standing position they may be able to use the paddle vertically as a support or crutch, resting in front of them on the centre line, or they may need more than one person helping. Holding the back of their buoyancy aid as you walk alongside a Supper in shallow water can stop backward falls.

One to one tuition, plus involving any of the students' regular helpers could be the best situation for some. Cost and lack of funding may be hurdles. There are charities that specialise in providing opportunities. If there are regular support workers who are competent Suppers it will help. I spoke with someone who works with people who have mental health issues. He was applying for funding from Sport England for equipment, but as instruction wasn't included they were looking to have staff trained in teaching SUP. As fluctuations in motivation can make scheduling external instructors difficult this was the most pragmatic option.

Sally Pugh has worked as a teacher at a school for pupils with learning difficulties or disabilities and also as a carer and now a playmaker for a children's hospice called Julia's House. With inspirational enthusiasm, she has much experience of involving groups and individuals in watersports and recommends:

● Focus on the person first and the impairment leading to the disability second.
● Have a 'can do' enthusiasm for allowing people the same opportunities.
● Include helpers and carers in the experience.
● A sense of fun and participation leads to a sense of achievement.
● Build trust and confidence with an adaptive and problem-solving approach.
● Communicate directly with people, even if helped by the carer.
● Relevant gestures or sign language are useful.

Helping and adapting the sport to be more inclusive has the potential to provide wonderfully uplifting experiences for many participants as well as for helpers, guides and instructors.

*Supping is a way to explore different environments.*

# Coaching kids

The Royal Yachting Association provides online training on safeguarding issues and good practice when working with children or vulnerable adults, called the 'Safe and Fun Safeguarding Course' with details on their website: rya.org.uk

Some people are very used to leading groups of children, but for others it may be a challenge. When I first started helping school groups with nature activities as an Assistant Ranger, I felt a bit of trepidation. I marvelled at the ease with which more experienced colleagues developed a rapport. This enabled me to observe a few pointers that helped. Some youngsters will be great at breaking down barriers, but often you have to encourage this. Once you know how to plan and lead a few activities including games and challenges it helps. Here are some tips:

● Give them attention, encouragement and praise.
● Learn names. (This is a skill in itself. There are memory systems where you picture an image with some connection to a name. For instance you imagine a girl called Holly with a few prickly leaves and red berries growing out of her head. The more bizarre, the more memorable. I try it with adults too. It worked well, until I introduced someone called Richard Limb to a group of people ... as Richard Thigh.)
● Have a plan but be flexible.
● Ask questions and give them a chance to shine. Some that don't excel in school lessons will be in their element, thus boosting their confidence. Active ones who struggle to sit down for long will prefer Supping to being in classrooms or even kayaks! Where youngsters feel disillusioned with school this may help them to become upstanding citizens and, who knows, possibly stand-up paddle instructors!
● Sometimes they'll come up with their own ideas and activities, and if safe let them.
● If the weather is warm, they'll often take pleasure from getting each other wet, but don't let them become too cold.
● MegaSups can accommodate several and develop team skills as well as being enjoyable to jump on and off.
● Remember SEA: safety comes first.
● Remain responsible until they all get back safely to their teacher, group leader or the correct parents/responsible adults.
● It can be good if teachers join you, particularly as they know what the individuals are like, but they won't always want to and children really appreciate a degree of independence.
● Don't undermine their school teachers, but have a quiet chat if there are issues.
● Smile, make it fun and have a laugh. Participate in some games, but retain

your inner maturity. Don't try so hard to be likeable that you lose all respect and control.

Sometimes they'll say things that delight or surprise you. I've also taught cycling to youngsters. With one group of nine-year-olds, I was particularly impressed with one girl called Rosie (to remember, you could imagine rose petals instead of hair). She had been born with only one lung. The school was in a hilly area, but while other children complained they were tired, she just toughed it out.

On the last of four two hour sessions, someone said a phrase that reminded me of a song. As you may have gathered, I like a lyric and semi-consciously sang a couple of lines. Rosie asked me, 'Why do you sing?' I answered cheerfully, 'That's a good question. I find it uplifting and that song came into my head.' She clarified, 'No, no, why do you sing - when you cannot sing?!'

To the above list add:

'Stay together you two!'

- Never underestimate them.
- Don't trust the little blighters!

As you become more confident, children will warm to you more readily and the more you'll feel comfortable. It's a virtuous circle, though I still take a deep breath as a coach-load arrive. Helping youngsters develop skills and confidence is incredibly worthwhile and rewarding, a real privilege.

Making do with a paddle for a canoe.

# ACKNOWLEDGEMENTS

Firstly, I would like to thank my colleagues with Easyriders, Andy Gratwick and Will King (now with RNLI), for teaching me about the sport. Along with Dave Hartwell of The Watersports Academy at Sandbanks Hotel, they have given me many opportunities to enthuse all manner of interesting, likeable people about this wonderful activity.

I owe much gratitude to all those who have given of their time and knowledge to check and contribute to chapters of the book: Allen Westerby, Roger Turner, Simmone Bristow, Sally Pugh, Rachel Woods, Andy Gratwick, Emma Rance, Anthony Ing, Pete Frith, Jonny Owen, Bill Morrison and Ben Seal. Any errors and opinions are mine.

Thanks must also go to all the friends who have paddled with me and taken part in photographs, often obliging in cold conditions or water. I'm also in awe of the skill and generosity of the many people who have let me include their photographs, either anonymously or credited to their work.

Thank you to my sister Helen for her knowledge of the book industry and for giving me the confidence to approach a publisher. I'm especially grateful to Jonathan Eyers, Sarah Jones and the team at Bloomsbury for always being so helpful and friendly, no matter how busy they are.

Finally, I'd like to say a huge 'thank you' to Heather for putting up with me wanting a paddle wherever we go.

(Nb. Every effort has been made to credit accurately. Any errors or omissions will be corrected at the first opportunity. Paintings are by the author.)

*Thank you!*

# APPENDIX

## Relevant reading

*How to Read Water*, Tristan Gooley, Sceptre 2017, 9781473615229

*Canoe and Kayak Games*, Dave Ruse and Loel Collins, Rivers Publishing 2005, 0955061407

*Reeds Nautical Almanac*, Mark Fishwick and Perrin Towler, Bloomsbury, updated annually

*What's Really Happening to Our Planet?* Tony Juniper, Dorling Kindersley 2016, 9780241240427

*The Tale of Squirrel Nutkin*, Beatrix Potter, Frederick Warne & Co. 1903/2002, 9780723247715

*Canoe and Kayak Map of Britain*, Rivers Publishing, 9780955061431

## SUP forums

There are a growing number of SUP-related forums to be found on Facebook, including: Stand Up Paddleboarding UK and Ireland; Stand Up Paddleboard UK; SUP hacks; SUPhubUK; TotalSUP; SUP and Paddlesports social meets and events; SUP Events in the UK; SUP Racing UK/Ireland/Channel Islands; SUP surfing UK and Ireland; SUP used boards for Sale England; SUP Boards for Sale UK and Ireland and Buy, Sell, Swap Standup Paddleboards UK.

# PICTURE CREDITS

# INDEX